BEGINNER'S GUIDE TO ECO RENOVATION

UNDERSTAND THE BASICS AND THE BEST QUESTIONS TO ASK

JUDITH LEARY-JOYCE

Produced and published in August 2022 by AoEC Press

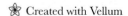 Created with Vellum

CONTENTS

ACKNOWLEDGEMENTS

First and foremost, thanks to Julia Healey[1], ARB, for her support and expertise. She gave her time so generously, reading through every word to make sure it was accurate and useful for the reader. I just couldn't – and wouldn't – have achieved this without her.

Other professionals gave their time to review chapters: Adam White and Vasilis Giannopoulos, Internorm[2]; Simon Robinson, Solinvictus;[3] Gian Vetere,[4] Domestic Energy Assessor. Thank you for giving me peace of mind.

To John, my husband, for reading, reviewing and endless discussions – two building bores together.

To Martha Dunlop[5], my daughter, for sharing her knowledge and experience in the practicalities of publishing.

Thanks to:

Suzanne Arnold[6] for her support, sensitive editing and making me laugh along the way.

Nadine Catto[7] for proof reading and teaching me about en–space.

Olinart[8] for my lovely cover and her patience as I nitpicked my way towards a final version.

Alexandra Peace[9] for persisting with the index and going the extra mile to sort me out when I messed up.

And to family and friends who put up with my enthusiasm for insulation and encouraged me to keep going.

———————————————————

1. https://clarenasharchitecture.co.uk/julia-healey/
2. https://www.internorm.com/en-uk/
3. http://solinvictus.co.uk
4. https://www.linkedin.com/in/gian-vetere-20981795/?originalSubdomain=uk
5. https://www.marthadunlop.com
6. https://www.suzannearnold.com/
7. https://www.nadinecattoeditorial.co.uk
8. https://www.fiverr.com/olinart
9. https://indexers.ca/acadp_listings/alexandra-peace/

FOREWORD

When Judith asked me to write this foreword, I struggled at first to know what to say. Thinking eco when planning home renovations and retrofit just seems obvious to me – both for the environment and our bills.

We're doing much better in considering our day-to-day impact, helped by a rising cost of living. So it's interesting that we don't automatically do the same when considering our homes.

Your house is probably the biggest investment you'll ever make. It's the place where you feel safe; the place where family is. So for something that important we need to do the very best we can.

There is plenty of information out there for those with knowledge, patience and an understanding of the technology. However, I've discovered that not everyone is as excited about fluid dynamics as I am – not sure why! So if you're one of those people then this book is perfect for you.

Working alongside Judith was really interesting for me. I enjoyed hearing a lay person explain complex issues in simple terms. And that's what this is – a simple summary of the process of eco renovation. It won't give you the answers, but it does provide an easy-to-understand overview so you can define your questions and know where to look for the answers you need.

Good luck with your eco house and thank you for doing what you can for the environment.

Julia Healey, BA(Hons), MA(Cantab), MArchD, ARB,

CHAPTER 1
INTRODUCTION

I f you are about to renovate, extend or update your home, I'd love you to make it a shining example of an eco home. You would immediately reduce your carbon footprint, contributing to a safer world for future generations, while reducing your energy bills and being distinctly more comfortable than before.

I've written this book to help you do just that, by sharing ideas and stories based on my experience of renovating and future-proofing a 1901 Victorian end-of-terrace house with the environment in mind. It gives an overview of the areas to be addressed, ideas for how to go about it, suggestions for who to contact and where to find what you need.

I am not an expert – just a fascinated amateur and eco-warrior, determined to make a difference. I can't give you all the answers, but I hope I can give you the confidence to ask all the questions you need.

I didn't do this on my own – I've had professional back up. I have been supported by Julia Healey, BA(Hons) MA(Cantab) MArchD ARB, an architect who specialises in retrofitting old houses. She read through the book in detail, correcting my mistakes and making suggestions for additions.

Where I stepped out of her specific expertise, I involved other experts who looked over the relevant sections, correcting and adding as appropriate.

I have included web links when I think they might be useful for more information. Some are business websites so they may have a sales element. **This is not an endorsement of the specific business** – just that what they wrote was interesting. Where people have been helpful to us and I'm happy to recommend, I have made that clear.

WHY THIS IS SO IMPORTANT

Our homes create 14% of the UK's carbon emissions.

Let's just take that in for a minute. 14%!

But we have made some progress: "The average UK home's carbon footprint has reduced by **4.7 tonnes of carbon dioxide since 1990**. A further reduction of **3.6 tonnes per household** by **2030** will help keep us on track to the 80% UK-wide reduction in emissions by 2050 required to tackle dangerous climate change[1]."

On the other hand, most of the UK's near-30 million homes are "not in a condition[2] to keep us comfortable and safe and productive in the changing climate", are "not going to be fit for us to live in" and "are a big part of causing the problem of climate change", according to Baroness Brown, chair of the Climate Change Committee (CCC).

And it seems that only 1% of new homes – built in a time when we know how damaging carbon emissions are to the environment – are completed with an EPC (Energy Performance Certificate) rating of A. So there is a very long way for the building profession and the government to go.

But you don't have to wait for that. If you are fortunate enough to own your home, then you have power in your hands – you can start making a difference now by:

- reducing your carbon footprint
- making your house cheaper to run
- addressing traditional UK issues of damp and poor ventilation
- using renewable energy.

You don't need to be an eco expert. You just need to understand enough to ask the right questions and explain any worries. As a result, this is a 'how-to-think-about-it' book, rather than a practical 'how-to-do-it' book.

There is one proviso: you really need to understand the link between insulation, airtightness, breathability and ventilation, otherwise you will store up problems for the future. So please read all these chapters before you start or as soon as you can. That way you'll be prepared for any questions or concerns you need to raise with your providers and you can avoid the dangers of addressing just one element on its own.

HOW TO USE THIS BOOK

You can think of the content as forming three sections:

Preparation for your project:

- getting clear on your priorities
- finding your support networks.

The work that needs to be done:

- insulation
- airtightness
- breathability
- ventilation
- heating and solar energy
- windows and doors.

The stuff that goes on around the build:

- finding energy-efficient appliances
- deciding on décor with eco in mind
- getting rid of surplus stuff without feeding landfill.

And a glossary of terms – a very important chapter for when you don't understand a word the builders/architects are saying or need the right words to go exploring online.

_____

1. https://www.theccc.org.uk/wp-content/uploads/2016/07/5CB-Info graphic-FINAL-.pdf
2. https://www.theccc.org.uk/2019/02/21/uk-homes-unfit-for-the-chal lenges-of-climate-change-ccc-says/

CHAPTER 2
YOUR HOME IS YOUR CASTLE

S o many people are improving homes: loft extensions, conservatories, refurbished kitchens, building new rooms, garden rooms… During covid we've stared at the walls – seeing all the cracks, hating the colours, feeling crowded by family or horribly isolated and just generally wanting this place we live in to feel more welcoming and attractive.

Great news for the economy, the building trade and happy homes. But also a huge opportunity for the environment. All it requires is to insulate, ventilate and heat in an earth-friendly way. But so few people are thinking of it. Why is that?

- First – it feels like a minefield. What does it involve? Do we need a special architect? Will the builder know the ropes? Will it make any difference?
- Second – the cost. Does it cost more and is it worth it?

YES – it will make a difference. And YES it will save you money. Now my husband John and I have had a full year in our eco'd house, we've been able to run the figures (based on kilowatt hours since cost changes regularly).

We used 75% less energy in the first year of the eco'd house, so our bills will be only 25% of our pre-renovation energy usage.

Yes, it may cost a bit more to do, but you choose how far you want to go – it is possible to do eco on a budget. Not to mention there will be long term savings in a well-insulated house plus a significant reduction in your carbon footprint.

It will help to have an architect and builders who know the ropes, who think about the environment as they work and have done it all before. But if you can't find or afford that, then you can inform yourself and work with your builder to deliver the output you want. The main challenge is to find providers who are willing to listen and learn with you.

IT'S ALL UP TO YOU

The cost and extent of the work are determined by the choices you make. Building regulations will take you so far but, looked at from an eco perspective, they are the minimum. There's a lot more you can do that will make a real difference to the state of your home and the state of the earth.

In my experience, there is a dearth of clear information about eco building. As a generalisation, most builders won't know much more than you do. They'll have done their job in a particular way for a long time and may not be interested in changing or learning. To build/develop eco-wise is a stretch and not everyone wants to be bothered. But if enough of us ask about additional insulation and how to manage ventilation, then builders will have to find a way to respond. We have purchasing power and now's the time to use it.

WHY WE WANTED TO FUTURE PROOF

Since the 1970s John and I have been climate-focused. We became Friends of the Earth as soon as Jonathan Porritt started it; we early adopted everything environmental, earning derision from some around us; I studied deep ecology with Joanna Macy, feeling the damage we're doing on a visceral level; we've marched; become veggie, now vegan; shaken tins to raise funds – all for as long as we can remember. I'm a plastic vigilante of the first order, so if you ever meet me please don't bring a plastic carrier bag or single use water bottle – I may have apoplexy!

We've lived in our 1901 end-of-terrace Victorian house for over 40 years and made many changes along the way. It looks small from the front but is a Tardis on the inside. When someone came to measure up for our kitchen, she called the office to check she was in the right place. "This house isn't big enough for the kitchen we've planned," she told her colleague. And then she came inside. It's an adventure of a house and all the more loved for it.

This latest renovation had been planned for a few years despite being a bone of contention. You know those 'discussions' that are constantly dumped in the 'too difficult' box? John wanted to take down the conservatory – lovely in the summer, freezing in the winter – and extend the kitchen onto the same footprint. I liked the idea – so much more light – but didn't want the extra drain on energy from an open-plan space in what was essentially a dark and chilly ground floor. Not to mention the fact that I hate having the builders in and moan my way through the entire process.

But soon I was hoist on my own petard. John realised I'd be more likely to move ahead if we went eco – we could get the extension done and benefit the earth along the way. Then our chosen builder popped in to say: "I can start next Thursday or no idea when it will be."

Well – what would you do? I just had to bite the bullet and get on with it.

SO ignorant!

With hindsight, we had no idea what we were doing. We'd done plenty of ordinary building, but this was a different kettle of fish and we didn't even realise until a few weeks into the project. And the realisation came a bit at a time, so we were constantly surprised and glued to the internet to find out what needed to happen next.

Our architect was good but focused on the extension, because that's all we thought we were doing. I can still feel the moment when the penny dropped. I suddenly realised that the new room was only the start and we'd have to retrofit our way back through the house. It sounds crazy now, but maybe it was a good thing. I may never have started if I'd really understood.

I also remember the moment when being resident moaner lost its charm. I could sulk loudly or knuckle down and get involved. I decided on the latter and really enjoyed it – as much as I'll ever enjoy living in a tiny space surrounded by dust and mess or cooking birthday goodies in a one-metre-square space with the occasional mouse joining in.

I want an air source heat pump

This was our starting point. John loves all things innovative and had been watching the progress of the air source heat pump (ASHP) for a long time. So this was his moment. He really wanted us to have one and my desire to go eco gave him all the permission he needed. So far so good.

The penny-dropping moment was driven by this decision. The architect pointed out that we'd need good insulation to make this possible and so the plans for the extension carried details of an eco-friendly wall construction that would give us what we needed to make the ASHP efficient... but only in the extension.

The penny – or gold bar – that dropped was realising that however well the extension was prepared for the ASHP, the heat would quickly be lost through the rest of our leaky old house.

From that moment on, it was endless discussions into the night, scribbling on large sheets of paper, concocting the next day's list of actions, endless hours online, calls to any expert we could muster, discussions with the builder, plumber, carpenter – most of whom thought we were a bit nuts...

But we explored, experimented, learned and finally built our way into a house that is much better insulated, well ventilated and considerably more comfortable than it was before. I know there are things we could have done better – which is very frustrating for a perfectionist – but it's as good as we could manage at the time.

Now I hope all that learning can prompt you to explore and discover your best options. If you're up for the challenge, that is: to take action on the climate crisis by making your own home more comfortable and cheaper to run than it was before.

What's not to go for?

CHAPTER 3
DEFINE YOUR APPETITE

Start with the fundamental questions: why are you doing this? How far do you want to go? What are your priorities? If possible, come to a conclusion before speaking with experts, builders, architects…

It's a conversation between you and your partner; you and the bank; you and your values. You need to decide what's important and the outcomes you want. You can work out most questions and challenges easily once you understand why you are doing what you're doing.

There are numerous reasons to work on your house:

- to give yourself more room and comfort
- to put right problems with damp, condensation, heating, bad DIY
- just plain can't stand the way the house looks now
- to increase the value of your investment and make the place more saleable
- to keep up with the neighbourhood
- to do your bit for the climate crisis
- just because you're fed up and want a new project.

All reasons are valid and you'll probably be driven by more than one. Think about it and decide what is most important so you're clear what you want, where to put your money and where to invest your time. Then once the questions and decisions start coming – and they'll come thick and fast most days – clear priorities will reduce the stress.

THE TOUCHSTONE

Knowing your priorities gives you a quick touchstone when the builder pops their head around the door to tell you:

- We should do it this way, because it's cheaper/easier/more convenient (but little consideration of environment or style).
- We can't get hold of those eco-materials you want, but we can get other stuff today from the local supplier, so let's do that so we don't lose time.
- I suggest we put pipes here – it's the easiest way – and we don't really need all that lagging.
- The insulation we've put in is fine. Building regs agree and if we do what you ask for it's going to take a lot longer. I think we just need to keep moving.

I bet you could put in your own specifics and answer happily while reading this in a peaceful setting. But I can assure you that when you're surrounded by dust and mess with hammer drills going hell for leather in the background, the answer is much less obvious. And it will happen more than once a day, that's for sure. So having that touchstone is more helpful than you can possibly imagine.

Elements of the touchstone

Define the different elements that are important to you and use these as the planks of your personal touchstone. The central ones are:

- Environment – are we going to make the climate crisis worse or better?
- Design – will it look the way we want it to look?
- Budget – how much will it cost and can we afford it?

Addressing the climate crisis is something we should all be mindful of. The effects are there for us to see if we just pay attention, so helping ourselves and those who follow is imperative.

There are different ways to do this. You can go the whole hog and make your home as near to carbon neutral as you can by using materials that are sustainable and don't use masses of energy in production (i.e. have low embodied energy) or you can create the same outcome with materials that are not sustainable and have high embodied energy.

Using sustainable products is the win–win of climate support. It means using products that don't deplete the earth and will eventually – in many many years – rot down and blend right back in. The downside is that they can cost a bit more and some of them take up more space – e.g. you may need a greater thickness of sustainable internal insulation.

If you can't manage this, then do what it takes to make sure your home uses as little carbon as possible. When the deliveries come in, wrapped in heavy plastic, clearly factory made and probably involving petrochemicals, it's not such a good feeling. But if this is the only way you can create the high levels of insulation and airtightness needed, then better go with it than to leave your home like a leaky bucket.

The remaining two elements – design and budget – are very closely linked to climate and environment, although it's easy to forget that. Design isn't just about what we want the place to look like. It's also about materials, manufacture, energy use, air miles etc. Everything you use will affect the climate in some way, so you have the choice to just go with the look or embark on an adventure to be as sustainable as your budget allows.

And budget is a very real issue for everyone. One of the reasons we're in the climate crisis is the desire to make everything cheap. Generally, the cheaper the item, the less sustainable it will be. But that is starting to change. Creative reuse, rehoming – all those fancy words for second hand – are quite rightly becoming fashionable. So take a look at chapter 15 on recycling – someone else's hand-on or bit of leftover building material could be your up-cycled treasure… you never know.

Our touchstone

Being eco-friendly was a condition of starting, so we had the first plank of our touchstone in place from the outset. Which was just as well. Given we didn't really understand what was involved it would have been so tempting to stick to the familiar – after all, we'd done extensions before and knew the score pretty well, whereas the eco way was outside everyone's comfort zone.

Within a couple of weeks we were starting to understand the challenge at hand, so we had the conversation to get clear about what we both wanted to do. We came down to the following prioritisation:

1. environment/climate
2. budget
3. design.

A great example was when the builder told us he was lining the soakaway with heavy plastic. Over my dead body! Turns out, once he looked into it, that it was perfectly acceptable to fill the hole with rubble and, since they'd just dug up the conservatory floor, we had plenty of that. I had to put up with raised eyebrows, but it worked fine and meant one less bit of plastic on the earth.

And then there was a really tough call when beautiful wall lights, that had taken many hours to find, wouldn't take LED bulbs. SO tempting just to accept it – after all, what difference would a couple of lights make? But we had our touchstone and that meant starting the search again. I suspect that we've now got a better option, but I did totally love those lights.

And of course, the insulation. The architect plans said to use Pavaflex in the new extension – a flexible wood fibre material that is eco-friendly. The builder was happy with PIR – a familiar, very popular insulation board made with chemicals and plastics. We had to decide who to go with at the outset and then, once we undertook to do the rest of the house, whether to continue as we'd begun.

Because our touchstone was clear, each question became a no-brainer. Which was just as well, really, since PIR (e.g. Kingspan) is a very effective insulation for its thickness, so we were committing to increased amounts of insulation for the same effect. If we hadn't worked it out between us, it would have been really tempting to take the easy option, but we knew it was more harmful to the earth and that contradicted the first point of our touchstone. There were a couple of places where we didn't have the luxury of more space, so we used PIR for those, but at least we could make an informed decision.

Touchstone alignment with your builder

Once your priorities are clear, it's easier to choose the most appropriate professionals – architects, engineers and builders. You need to work with people who understand your priorities and are happy to work with them. Ideally find someone who has similar values then, if you're not around, you're more likely to be happy with the choices they make.

It's so important that the people you employ really understand what matters to you and what that means in reality. When it comes to eco building this isn't a slam dunk. We all have different views about what 'eco' means and different standards we adhere to. You only need to walk around the roads and look at what people put in skips to realise that. Even people who say they care about the environment dump surprising stuff – cardboard that can be recycled, furniture with life left in it and toys that could be passed on or upcycled. And if your builders don't have similar standards you'll end up like John, very frustrated, sorting out the skip after they've gone home each day.

These conversations take time but can avoid problems down the line. We made too many assumptions about mindsets, beliefs and how effective our own communication was. It cost us in support: with the architect who didn't take in just how serious we were; with our builder, where we made assumptions about shared eco concerns; and with endless tradespeople, who looked for shortcuts where that was the last thing we wanted. By the end, they would all reference the eco elements because they finally got it, but we could have made our life easier and inspired greater concern if we'd over-communicated and made no assumptions.

APPETITE FOR ADVENTURE

It's also helpful to analyse your spirit of adventure and work with people who match it. Just as we consider our appetite for risk when investing money, it's a great idea to review willingness to experiment or try new ideas when renovating.

I'm slow on the uptake with different or unusual ideas. Given I have a husband who has 10 ideas when one would do perfectly well, this leads to some frustrating conversations. But then, once I'm on board, I'm really on board – which makes me pretty irritating. Don't persuade me, then backtrack. If we need something particular, I'll do everything I can to sort it out, even if that means we have to wait or deviate from the plan.

If you love new ideas and want to make decisions as you go along, then the conversation with your builder needs to focus on flexibility and willingness to explore options. John will question everything and come up with new solutions to the most intractable problem. It's driven me wild over the years when I just want to get on, but I've learned that most times he finds a solution, so I have developed faith in his ability to sort stuff out. I've also learned that he'll back off his idea easily if presented with good reasons why it won't work – he just agrees and starts again.

So we needed a builder who wasn't wedded to their own way. Fortunately, we found Pete, who understood that and took loads of time to talk and try options – like finding a different way to do the soakaway. I'm sure there were times when he thought we were totally over the top, but it was our home and our choice, so as long as he could see the decision was robust he went with us.

If you don't like adventure, then your conversation probably needs to focus on the practical. You'll want to be quite sure you can trust your builders to do a good job, to include you when needed and to let you alone when they are on the case. You don't want long discussions about options, just clear information and advice about the best way ahead. It's a fine balance, so is worth taking the time to sort out – you want them to be proactive, without excluding you, so get clear in your mind how much involvement you want and how you can go about getting it.

WHAT YOUR BUILDER NEEDS FROM YOU

Having put thought into what *you* want, take time out with your builder to find out what *they* need from you in order to do their best job.

It became clear as we went along that I am the planner. Every day I had a list to work through. Every day I was trying to understand who was going to do what when and what I had to do to be ready for them. This was how I managed John and his idea factory. Turns out it was also useful to Pete. Because he works on one project at a time, he has his own style and loads of information in his head that rarely sees the light of day. He knows exactly what he's doing and just gets on with it. But then we interrupted that process by deciding to retrofit the rest of the house, so something different was needed.

In retrospect, I realise I became something of a project manager. In the new scenario, Pete needed to understand what we wanted and I had to understand what our requirements meant to him and what he needed from us as a result.

So each day, I'd start with my list and check it through with him. He'd correct assumptions, provide contacts we needed and ask questions when he wasn't clear. So, eventually, we got a system going. It wasn't without its challenges, but it worked overall.

TO STAY OR NOT TO STAY

I must admit, it never occurred to us that we might move out while the work was being done. I know lots of people do these days and it is certainly a great deal more comfortable, but we've done this a number of times and always stayed, so we just did the same again.

We managed to leave the front room and our bedroom out of the equation (at the start, anyway) so we had a retreat, albeit stuffed with furniture, general gubbins and muck. Turns out it's difficult to clean while edging your way around a room! I cooked in a tiny space with my hat and coat on while we were without windows and doors, but still managed to do BreadAhead[1] cooking classes online. My Christmas mince pies were the best yet and Amaretti biscuits will forever remind me of concrete, dust and insulation.

When we finally gave in – just too much dust and too many trades at one time – and moved in with our daughter over the road, we realised how lovely it was to have clean space around us. We went for one week and stayed for a month – a peaceful interlude in a vortex of mess.

There are pros and cons, of course.

Staying: pros

- Saves money on rent, so more money for doing the work you want.
- You stay in touch with progress and the standard of work on a day-to-day basis.
- When you live with what is being done in real time, you may spot options that you didn't think about in theory.
- You know about it as soon as something is no longer needed and can therefore pass it on sustainably.
- You have a more intimate relationship with the deeper details of your home – e.g. how the heating system works; where electrics and pipes are situated etc.

Staying: cons

- Pretty unpleasant – dirty and dusty.
- Builders have to work around you, which may mean not doing things the easiest and quickest way.
- Builders have to clean up for you at the end of each day, which takes time.

Moving out: pros

- Considerably more comfort once the move is done. Treat it as an adventure and you can have a good time in another home.
- Space for the builders to sequence the work in a way that is easier for them. They also don't have to tidy up at the end of each day.

Moving out: cons

- Cost – you are funding another residence as well as your own.
- If the build runs late, you're less able to put pressure on/builders don't see the impact of their tardiness.
- You feel more distant from the whole process (depending on your view, you might see this as a huge pro!).

SUMMARY

- Work out what matters most to you: budget, climate/environment, design. Knowing this will help with day-to-day decision making.
- Consider the issue of sustainability. Going with it is the win–win of climate protection. If you can't, make

your house energy efficient in whatever ways you can, rather than leaving it in a leaky state.

- Talk with your builder, architect, designer… to make sure their touchstone aligns with yours and they fully understand what matters to you. Be prepared to overdo this, to make sure you are fully understood – better to be safe than sorry.

- Decide on your appetite for adventure – are you willing and able to change course mid-build or does it need to follow the plan – both for your sanity and your budget. Again, make sure your builder understands your view.

- Decide whether you want to carry on living in the property as the work continues or move out to somewhere more comfortable.

---

1. http://www.breadahead.com/elearning

CHAPTER 4
FIND YOUR COMMUNITY

We didn't know what we didn't know. This was the biggest challenge at the outset and we had no idea what to ask of who.

It often came down to a single fact that, if we'd known or understood it, would have made our life a lot simpler. A perfect example was not realising that we were 'retrofitting'. Sounds daft now, as I write it, but just knowing that word would have opened up a whole world online.

Another one was understanding about ventilation. I came across heat exchange ventilation units by accident, and it clarified something we really needed to know. We could have ended up with a whole range of problems if we'd missed that one.

Even now, we're discovering stuff – like finally understanding the difference between insulation and airtightness. But that's a story for another chapter…

Like much in life, it's more often about the questions we ask than the knowledge we have. Once you know the right question you can invariably find the answer.

YOUR COMMUNITY

My lovely daughter told me in no uncertain terms that I'd become a building bore. I apologised politely, not at all sure she was right. Then, one day, someone answered a Freegle ad and when they came to pick up our spare tiles we ended up sharing experiences for a good hour, despite the necessary cold, 'covid-safe' garden location. I had met another building bore and I can't tell you how happy I was! My daughter was right after all!

I'm sure you can recognise times when your community has been invaluable. When getting married, every bride or groom is a godsend; when you have a new baby, all you want is another sleep-deprived parent to talk to about green nappies; when planning an extension, you become endlessly fascinated by planning permission. And when you start the building process, life is defined by taps, bricks and window frames. And you desperately need another person with the same sharp focus.

So make it a priority to find out where your community is located.

Facebook renovations pages

Go onto Facebook[1] and search for 'home renovation groups near me'. Someone is sure to have set up a page to help them find like-minded souls and each page will be a fount of wisdom.

Our local Facebook page is remarkable – ideas, suppliers, paint colours, insulation, hinges – whatever you want to know, someone else will have asked it before you and been given a range of answers. All you have to do is use the search facility. If that doesn't provide what you want, then post your question and invariably you'll have an answer within a couple of hours.

Other building bores are very generous with their time and knowledge.

And one day the wonderful moment will arrive when you are the one answering questions. How exciting is that! Not just that you've learned about renovation. It also means you are at the end or nearing the end of your own mess and shambles. Life is beginning to return to a new normal and you are ready to help others. And that, my friend, is complete magic.

A good social media page of this type is usually well managed so check the rules first. You need to know if suppliers are allowed to promote their skills or wares or whether it is purely for those engaged in renovating their own homes. The latter is far preferable because recommendations are made from direct experience, with no advertising hype or picture of perfection. If you hear of a tradesperson who sounds good, you can check out if someone else has used them or is recommending them. We found some good people that way.

If the forum focuses on the positive, you may find that people don't speak clearly about the negatives, which might be a bit of a problem. In that case, the absence of a response can be a prompt to think again and search further. Or use direct messages (DM) to ask specific questions of other customers so you can check out a tradesperson.

Search for local environmental groups

What you're looking for is other eco-concerned people who are doing their own building work, so begin by searching for groups near you – 'sustainability' is a great word to start with. Our local sustainability group is an umbrella for many different aspects of environmental and community work, so reaching into groups like that from any angle can start you on a journey of discovery. For example, you could try some of the following:

- Re-wilding Britain[2] – groups coming together to support gardeners to make habitats for wildlife
- Climate assembly UK[3] – bringing people together to talk about how the UK can reach its climate targets
- Playing Out[4] – support if you want to close your road so the kids can play outside like we used to in the 'olden days'.

I realise these options aren't directly about eco homes. However, if it's not immediately obvious where your eco people are, go to where they are most likely to hang out and ask around. Remember the rules of networking – you're never more than six moves away from the person you need.

ECO RENOVATION BOOKS

We tried to find relevant publications to help us out, but because we didn't have the right terminology we weren't very successful. We found a great book once we'd finished – of course we did!

- ***Old House Eco Handbook: A Practical Guide to Retrofitting for Energy Efficiency and Sustainability***[5] by Marianne Suhr and Roger Hunt: was recommended to us as the bible. A generous architect – Jaina Valji from Clare Nash Architecture[6] – assumed we must have the book already but gave us the name just in case.

With this book in our sticky mitts, we had to face the mistakes we'd made and the clear information we had failed to find in time. We did also have moments of true delight, however, when we found that we'd worked out the right thing to do all on our own.

The book covers retrofitting houses from the 16th century onwards, so some of it may not be relevant to you, but there is masses of knowledge and information that will, at the very least, set you on the right track to find the answers you need.

Here are some others we found:

The Environmental Design Pocketbook[7] by Sofie Pelsmakers: Sofie has a PhD in building energy demand reduction so really knows what she is talking about. The book is full of detailed information, so if you want to understand the mechanics and theories behind all this, this will be up your street. She also writes a very interesting blog if you want to discover more about eco building.

- ***Eco-House Manual***[8] by Nigel Griffiths: This is an old but useful book that gives detailed information about all the different elements of eco renovation. You will find information about reed-bed composting, air source heat pumps, sustainable flooring… right through to setting up a wind turbine. Make sure you get the most recent edition (2012 as I write), since this field is changing at a great pace.
- ***Converting to an Eco-friendly Home***[9] – ***the complete handbook*** by Paul Hymers: Another useful book with good diagrams that takes you through small and larger changes to the home. As with the *Eco-House Manual*, it was published a while ago – 2006 – so technology will have evolved quite a bit in that time. However, if you are keen to build a background understanding before you get going, this could help you.
- ***EnerPHit A step-by-step guide to low-energy retrofit***[10] by James Trainer: EnerPHit is the Passivhaus standard for retrofits. It's rigorous and challenging and won't be for everyone, but if you do

want to go down that route, this book may help. The main point is that the EnerPHit[11] process begins long before you get on site so begin your research straight away or you might miss the boat. The book was published in 2019. I think it is brilliant for architects and those studying for Passivhaus accreditation. Sadly it was too detailed and specific for us, so not a great help. It may be useful if your builder is interested to learn and become more actively involved.

I looked on Facebook and there is plenty of stuff on there about EnerPHit, but not one specific page. However, if you are really interested, it might be a good place to start looking for your people.

EXPERTS WHO CAN HELP

- **Centre for Alternative Technology**[12] (CAT): If you need advice from a source that isn't trying to sell you anything, try the CAT website. It has all sorts of information to set you thinking. And they were very helpful whenever we called them for advice. You will find all you need to know about being sustainable, from composting toilets to solar energy and all points in between.
- **Ecological Building Systems**[13]: Another very helpful organisation. They actually sell what you need if you are aiming at using green options, but even if you don't buy directly from them, we found them to be very open to a conversation and pointing us in the right direction.

In general, we found plenty of eco professionals who were happy to talk once they heard what we were trying to do. At present so few people are paying attention to building and the environment that I think we must have been music to their ears. So it's always worth asking. Remember – you're only six steps away – so have a go. Ask and you never know who or what you might find.

Finding your providers

This is never an easy call with pros and cons on all sides. There are certain points I try to keep in mind:

- When considering a large company, their sales team will always paint you a perfect picture. Whether they check feasibility with the people who actually have to deliver on the promise is another matter. However much you want to believe it will be as straightforward as they say, make sure you do the checking yourself and read the small print very thoroughly.
- When you're talking to a small provider, the person selling to you is more likely to be the one doing the work so they may be more realistic.
- Local providers are more likely to have direct knowledge of planning, building inspectors etc, so their personal relationships might be a real benefit to you.
- Talk about climate at the outset and see how they respond.
- Resist the temptation to rush. You may be put on the spot to make a quick decision, but people will always wait and better to wait than regret.

Whoever is doing the work, make sure they understand your touchstone priorities. The different areas of eco renovation will always overlap. So any pipes entering the building from your solar and/or ASHP, for example, will be a risk to airtightness and/or the insulation. As ever, don't assume people think the same way you do or take the big picture into account. Just make sure you underline what is important – take nothing for granted.

Architects

If you find a good eco-minded architect they will be worth their weight in gold. Work out ahead of time how much you are willing to pay for their help because anything beyond the initial plans will be an extra cost. However, if that extra cost stops you wasting money in other areas then it will be worth it.

Essentially, you need to set out a working brief. Best done at the outset, you can either produce it together or the architect will write it with reference to your requirements. It is a clear statement of what you want, what the architect will do and how you will work together. You can then refer back to the brief throughout the design process and your architect will do the same. It means your architect understands what you need and want and you can ask for help and suggestions when needed.

The alternative is that you might both be politely holding back when a little help would be invaluable. We'd have been happy to pay for more advice and help from our architect, but he didn't realise we needed it and we never thought to ask – a missed opportunity all round.

SUMMARY

- Keep looking for your community – having people around to chat to, exchange stories with and learn from is worth its weight in gold.
- Social media can be a good source of contact – Facebook groups for local homeowners, Instagram and Pinterest for design ideas. Use the internet liberally to help you.

- There are interesting books out there, but not so much that is up to date – that I found, anyway.
- Expert organisations can be very helpful – they enjoy supporting homeowners doing their best for the environment.
- Use your architect if you can – they will have all the information at their fingertips and they know your house.

---

1. https://www.facebook.com
2. http://www.rewildingbritain.org.uk/rewilding-network/projects
3. http://www.climateassembly.uk
4. https://playingout.net
5. https://www.waterstones.com/book/old-house-eco-handbook/roger-hunt/kevin-mccloud/9780711239777
6. https://clarenasharchitecture.co.uk/?sfw=pass1641816104
7. https://www.waterstones.com/book/environmental-design-pocketbook/sofie-pelsmakers/9781859465486
8. Eco-House Manual
9. https://www.abebooks.co.uk/9781845374068/Converting-Eco-friendly-Home-Complete-Handbook-1845374061/plp
10. https://www.waterstones.com/book/enerphit/james-traynor/9781859468197
11. http://www.passivhaustrust.org.uk/news/detail/?nId=992
12. https://cat.org.uk
13. https://www.ecologicalbuildingsystems.com

CHAPTER 5
WHERE TO START

First, understand the terminology for what you're going to do. This may not sound important, but having the right words is central to successful internet research.

You will either be:

- **renovating** – returning your home to a good state of repair by replacing old systems: rewiring, new plumbing, redecorating and/or modifying an existing home by adding extensions or loft rooms
- **retrofitting** – working your way through the house, putting in new systems that were not in place when the house was built in order to make it more efficient: solar panels, insulation, new heating systems...

Renovation is the most commonly used word, but retrofit is creeping in more as we consider how to future-proof our houses, helping the environment along the way.

Chances are, like us, you'll be doing both. The decision to build on a new kitchen or refurbish the ground floor (renovation) provides the perfect opportunity to insulate, ventilate and make airtight (retrofit). If you've got to move all your furniture anyway, why not insulate under the floors while you're at it? The two jobs go perfectly together.

So add in the word retrofit when doing your research – you may find more eco information comes up as a result.

WHAT DOES BEING ECO MEAN?

This is the big question. I assumed it was going to be a long list of things to do that would take years, pain and a lot of money. It's true there is a lot to do but, in essence, being eco comes down to:

1. Finding the most efficient, environmentally friendly way to produce heat: gas versus renewables.
2. Making sure your house can hold onto the heat once you've produced it: insulation.
3. Cutting out draughts – airtightness.
4. Making sure you have fresh air to breathe and reduce humidity: ventilation.
5. Managing condensation and mould: breathability.

And don't forget your touchstone – consider the materials you use. Will they come from renewable sources or non-renewable? How much energy has been expended on their production and transport?

Of course, under each of those headings are a number of questions, but still the top-level list is pretty short. Once I got hold of that, it all became easier. A bit like the touchstone, I found it useful to know we had five areas to cover, so I could focus on getting my head around those five and understand what they meant in our house.

For us this meant:

- Deciding how to produce heat – the desire for an air source heat pump (ASHP) was a big driver in us doing the work at all, so that was already a given.
- Reviewing the whole house for levels of insulation – we found it was pretty poor. We'd made a few half-hearted attempts over the years, but nothing like the level we actually needed.
- Addressing the draughts that were all around us – not for nothing was I the cashmere queen! We had cold feet and numerous jumpers for most of the year.
- Understanding the implications of breathability so we used the appropriate materials.
- Learning about ventilation – this had never been an issue before and struck us like a thunderbolt. If we cut out the draughts, we'd have a whole new issue to deal with. Nice problem to have, though.

The final piece was the decision about sustainable materials versus more conventional materials that were familiar and easy to access. Needless to say, our touchstone meant we went for sustainable wherever we could.

IMPORTANT – the 'big four' all work together

You can't address the issues of insulation, airtightness, ventilation and breathability in isolation. They all interconnect, so to be really energy efficient you need to weave them in together.

If you insulate without airtightness, you'll be disappointed. Insulation won't stop the draughts so you'll still feel chilly.

If you insulate and get airtight, but don't ventilate, the air will feel stale and you'll invite condensation and maybe mould.

If you live in an old house, leaving breathability out of the equation will also promote condensation and mould.

So please – read all four of these chapters before you start. Recognising the connection between the different elements will make your life so much easier and give you a much better outcome.

HOUSE CONSTRUCTION

Understanding the construction of your house is fundamental and defines how to go about addressing the big four questions.

For example, the concrete floors of a new build are draught-proof, but very cold and take a long time to warm up, even if they are well insulated; by contrast, the suspended floors of old houses are extremely draughty but can be insulated fairly easily.

Solid-wall houses

Ours is the perfect example of a solid-wall house: Victorian end of terrace with one vast unprotected external wall – in our case, facing east – so very cold.

Uninsulated solid walls are often cold. Imagine the external wall as an extension of 'outside' because it is always in contact with the outside air. When there is only one brick between you and the garden, the cold is transferred through the brick to the inside of the house. And when the warm air inside the house hits that cold brick, it cools, dropping any moisture it was holding. That's when you can get problems with condensation/damp and mould. You need to find a way to add in a second warm skin of some sort, so that cold air is held in the outer layer and warm air in the house only comes into contact with a warm internal surface.

Challenges that go along with solid-wall houses are:

- Single-brick walls throughout, bringing cold from the air directly into the house.
- Suspended timber floors that channel draughts from air bricks and damaged brickwork.
- Poorly organised ventilation (although this does allow for plenty of fresh air).
- Single-glazed windows, which become increasingly leaky over time.
- Chimneys – open or closed and vented: major cold-air channels.
- Loft – may be accessible, but the amount of insulation and quality of loft hatch can vary.
- Previous renovations, which meet outdated standards so are less efficient.
- Gas central heating, which was probably added as the most cost-effective option at the time but is now known to be very unfriendly to the environment as well as expensive.

If your house is in a conservation area that might limit what you're allowed to do. However given the climate emergency, the rules for these areas are beginning to move away from just the look of the place to consideration of the sustainability of the building. For example, we have finally been able to put solar panels on the roof despite being in a protected area, so don't be put off – keep checking and challenge the council on what is acceptable. (See chapter 6 – planning.)

Cavity wall houses

Cavity walls were introduced in the 1920s, so if your house was built after that, there is a chance this is what you have. Some houses from the 1920s and 1930s have a combination of cavity walls and solid brick, so it's important to find out exactly how your house was built. Cavity walls are relatively easy to fill with polystyrene or wood fibre for a first level of insulation, which makes an immediate difference to the warmth of your house.

The challenges that go along with cavity wall houses are:

- Cavity walls lying empty, or partially filled cavities where the insulation has sunk.
- Filled cavities that have leaked during DIY work or the insulation may have 'clumped', leaving some areas without protection.
- Single-glazed windows. Many have now been double-glazing, but efficiency will vary according to age.
- Floors may be wooden and suspended (draughty) or concrete, without insulation (cold.)
- Home improvements over time will have made for warmer houses, but lack of care over ventilation invites condensation and mould.

What about new houses?

You might expect a new home to be built to a high level with regard to eco performance.

All new builds should achieve an A rating on the Energy Performance Certificate (EPC). However, although some new houses do reach that standard, the vast majority are rated as B and some come as low as C. (See chapter 6 for more information) So if you have a new house there may still have some issues to address.

All new houses will have cavity walls and good insulation. The best will have been built as eco homes; others will have apparently followed the directives, but in fact speed and budget have been the touchstones, so they are now either leaky or struggling with condensation.

So if you're in a new house and ready to extend or remodel, you need to ask questions about:

- whether the cavity walls have been effectively insulated and the insulation remains in good condition
- quality of the double-glazed windows included in the build and their present condition
- form of heating and its efficiency – this will most commonly be gas central heating, but the type of boiler will determine how warm you are and how high your costs will be
- effectiveness of the flooring – you'll know this from how cold your feet get when walking barefoot or in your socks
- levels of condensation and/or mould, plus the style of ventilation that was included at the outset.

Condensation can be a big issue in airtight buildings, so needs particular attention in a new build, which is less likely to have draughts. It can be sorted out by putting in the correct amount of ventilation. You can read more about this in chapter 10.

SUMMARY

- Research both renovation and retrofit – this will give you lots more information.
- Consider the five steps of eco renovation to understand exactly what you need to do.
- Understand the structure of your house to identify the main areas to address in your eco renovation.
- Refer back to your touchstone to decide how to go about it.

CHAPTER 6
PLANNING AND BUILDING CONTROL

I f you're anything like me, you find planning the least exciting part of the build. It's a matter of effort and paperwork, patience as the process grinds slowly on its way, and possibly decisions about changes that you'd prefer not to make. Such a long way from the delight of a new home or even the fun of seeing the walls go up and plugs go in. However, we all have to bite the bullet and get on with it to make sure we have a build that is legal and appropriate.

The first question is whether you need planning permission at all or whether your plans fall within permitted development. For the short answer – it depends whether you're going to change the exterior of your house. If so, then you probably need planning permission.

The long answer is that you're going to have to check all your plans whatever. Your architect or builder should have a clear view of what's required. If you are working with an architect, they will probably manage the whole planning process on your behalf, which can be a massive relief, since they understand how it works and are up to date with local policy.

This is vital to your peace of mind and stress levels because planning policies are updated periodically and vary from one area to another. And for this reason, I won't be including specific details here – if you're reading the book even a few weeks after I wrote it, things may already be different. So I'll stick with a broad outline so you at least understand the different steps and what you need to do when. Once you've read this, then it's time to visit your local council website to find the specifics for your area.

First of all, there are different types of permission and agreement needed, depending on the nature of your build:

1. permitted development
2. planning permission
3. building regulations
4. party wall agreement.

PERMITTED DEVELOPMENT

This is work you are allowed to do without getting planning permission – hurrah! The rules for permitted development (PD) are quite particular so you'll need to go online and look into the specifics.

There are a number of developments that could be included:

- certain extensions depending on size and position (e.g. on the rear of the property)
- some loft conversions
- some garage conversions
- small porches and garden rooms
- internal alterations
- solar panels
- air source heat pumps
- roof lights or dormer windows

- new drives, depending on the drainage.

There are restrictions on the size and proximity to the boundary for some types of development. Never take anything for granted – always check online and with your local planning authority to make sure you have the most up-to-date information.[1]

If you live in a designated area such as a conservation area or Area of Outstanding Natural Beauty, you may find that your permitted development rights have been removed. If this is the case, you'll need to apply for planning permission for any planned works.

You can also apply for a Lawful Development Certificate, which can be helpful both for peace of mind and when you come to sell your property. It states clearly that the work you are going to carry out falls within the rules of permitted development so is a lawful confirmation of what you've done for future buyers.

Prior approval: Larger extensions may require something called prior approval, which involves an application to the council. A prior approval application is more straightforward and cheaper than a planning application, but the decision period is the same as for a planning application and it is publicly visible online.

Pre-application advice: Some councils offer a pre-application advice service. This gives you informal advice from a planning officer, and the pre-application is not made public, in the way a planning application would be. If you think something about your plans might be contentious, or you want to test a scheme with the planners without the entire neighbourhood knowing about it, then a 'pre-app' is very useful.

The pre-app process varies between councils, and some don't offer the service at all, so visit your local council website to find out exactly how to apply. Usually you'll be asked to submit a location plan and other relevant information such as floor plans and elevations. The advice can be given in a meeting, a written report or both. Again, it depends on your council which of these options will be available to you.

Be aware: there is no statutory time limit on pre-apps, so you could end up waiting a long time for a response if the planning department is over-stretched.

PLANNING PERMISSION

Remember this is only about the external appearance of your house – so we're talking about changes to the outside or the addition of extensions. The only time when inside might be relevant to planning is when you want to change the windows in some way or if what you're doing inside will impact the outside of the house.

There may also be additional restrictions placed on you if your house is in a conservation area or is a listed building. You'll find more details about this on the local council website.

———

Pretty street? Climate crisis? Which trumps which?

I've wanted solar panels for years, but we live in a conservation area so this was never a possibility. Also our house faces east–west, so I just reconciled myself and looked longingly at everyone else's panels.

Then came the day when the council declared a climate emergency. I was there to hear it happen and I remember our one Green councillor saying to the crowd standing at the back: "Hold us to account. I want to see you back here in six months demanding to know what we've done."

That stuck with me, so shortly afterwards I wrote to him asking the question: now you have accepted there is a climate emergency, which trumps which? A good-looking street or solar panels producing sustainable energy? I got a letter back pretty quickly encouraging me to keep asking the question and confirming that he would be pushing for solar on our behalf.

So when we were planning this recent renovation/retrofit, I wrote again to our own councillor. Two days later I got an email from her to say that my timing was great – the rules had just been changed. Now houses in conservation areas could have solar panels with just a few minor restrictions that were easy to accommodate.

So sometimes those regular changes are in our favour – keep checking and keep asking the questions!

———

There are a number of steps in the process and I'll give rough timelines for each step. This is the ideal – absolutely not written in stone – so manage your expectations by checking the reality in your area. This is something your architect or builder should be able to help you with.

Step one: submitting the application. Once you've refined the plans with your architect, they will put in an application to your local council planning office.

Step two: validation of the application (two weeks). The council will accept the application and begin an eight-week consultation process.

Step three: consultation with interested parties (21 days of the eight-week period). Letters will be sent to your neighbours, and notices put on lampposts in your road and other affected areas, giving information about where the plans can be viewed and a final date for commenting or objecting. Other interested parties that might be included are: environmental protection, conservation officer, ecology officer, the parish council, local interest groups etc, all of whom might want to see the plans. During this consultation period any of the affected people have the right to ask questions or lodge a complaint.

Step four: your architect will find out what's happening (five remaining weeks of the eight-week period). Once the 21-day consultation period is over, the agent (usually the architect, but whoever made the application) should contact the planners and find out what issues have been raised, whether any further information is required and whether any changes to the plans are recommended. This gives them the opportunity to make any necessary amendments to issues that might cause the application to be turned down.

Step five: visit from the planning officer (during the eight-week timeframe). The planning officer may decide to visit at any time during the eight-week period to verify the plans. If the relevant area can be seen clearly from the road, then you may never know it happened, so don't worry if you don't get a visit. If there is some question and they need to see the site, then they will arrange a suitable time. Remember this is only about the outside of your house, so it's possible it might be done even though you're not there.

Step six: final decision (eight weeks after the date on the validation letter). After all this has been done, a final decision will be made about whether your application is approved.

The cost of the application is a few hundred pounds and in an ideal world the whole process would take place over a two-month period, although I expect it often takes longer. Do find out about the local timeframe so you can apply in time and be ready to get going when you want to without being held up by the bureaucratic process.

Role of the architect

Having an architect involved at this point can be very helpful. When it comes to planning permission they are on familiar ground, whereas you may have no idea where to start. They will have in mind the rigours of the planning department throughout the design phase and will know what might be contentious and what's likely to go through easily. They are constantly managing the boundary between what you want and what they know will be acceptable to the planning department.

They'll send in a detailed pack of information with the planning application, after having shown it all to you. It's very important that you go through this with a fine-tooth comb – to make sure the plans really will give you what you want and to make sure any eco materials you've asked for are included. And not least because, once it is submitted, it will appear online for everyone to see.

Once you've finalised and agreed the plans with your architect, you can sit back and let them get on with it. Best practice will see them checking in with the planning officer during the consultation period to explore any problems. Planning people are generally very helpful so having an architect who will work with them can be a real boon.

When planning permission is refused

This is the point when the relationship between your architect and the planning officer is key. There are three possible options:

Option one: the planning officer makes clear to your architect during the consultation period that the application won't be accepted and they discuss adjustments that can be made. There may be time for your architect to make the changes before the application is decided or, if there are substantial changes to be made, you may decide to withdraw the application and submit a new one once all the issues have been resolved.

The council will usually give you the option of withdrawing the application if they know it will be refused it as it stands. When there are clear reasons for the application to be refused, withdrawal is usually the best option for all parties. The planners can avoid the paperwork involved in a refusal and you can avoid a hard 'no' in black and white for the work you want to do. It is very likely that when you resubmit your application you'll be assigned the same planning officer because they'll be familiar with the site, so a good relationship with them can go a long way.

Option two: your plans are refused. Now you can discuss options with the architect. You will have to adjust the plan and revise the proposal to remove the problem, then resubmit. If your proposal is on the same site and you can send it in again within one year, then this second application is free.

Option three: if your plans are refused and you don't want to accept the required changes, then you can appeal[2] the decision. Your refusal will come with a written report, mentioning all the reasons for the refusal and the policies that would be contravened. There is no fee for an appeal, but you have to prepare yourself for a very long-winded process.

Given you are reading a book about renovating your house, you would probably be involved in a householder appeal, which is a fast-track system for minor works such as loft conversions or extensions. This can take in the region of 16 weeks, although do check before you take the decision to do this.

It's very unlikely that planners will visit after planning approval has been granted – they won't try and surprise you or 'catch you out'. However, your neighbours may complain if you do something different from the approved plans, especially if they didn't like the whole idea in the first place.

———

The Granpad

Our previous renovation was a big deal planning-wise because we wanted to put a new hall on the side of the house. The kids had left home and it was time to create a Granpad (the aging version of a bachelor pad). The plan was to gut the ground floor and build into the side garden so we could remove the original hall wall and make the front room more spacious.

Plans went in and it seemed to be going well until a visit from the planning/conservation officer. She was very pleasant but clearly not happy. Finally she said, "If I could refuse you, I would. Once this is done, you will have wrapped the whole house in extensions." She was clearly concerned about the heritage of the house and I did see her point.

I'd always have said I love original features but she made me realise that my love is conditional. I also want my home to be light and bright. I don't want low ceilings where I bang my head or corners that are difficult to keep clean. I guess the truth is, I love original features in other people's homes.

Mind you, we had made great efforts, with the help of planning and the architect, to ensure the new hall fitted the front of the house so people walking past wouldn't notice a difference and I think we did a really good job. We'd mimicked the lovely arch above the door, got old brick so it matched up, kept the stained glass door... All of which meant the planning permission was granted, despite the officer's reservations, and we could take the next step in building our Tardis in the making.

BUILDING REGULATIONS

Complying with building regulations is the next step in having full permission to build. Just to be clear about the difference between the two:

- **planning permission** assesses the external elements of the build plus the impact on the local environment and authorises you to carry out the development
- **building regulations** cover the structural aspects of the build and track progress during the construction, ensuring it complies with the standards of construction.

Planning permission and building regulations approval are completely different – two separate pieces of legislation. Sometimes you need both, sometimes you may only need one or none at all. Please always check thoroughly to understand your specific requirements. There are real problems when you don't have the correct permissions, at worst having to take down what you've so lovingly built, so don't be tempted to rush over this part.

When applying for building regulations approval there are two options. You can:

One: go for full plans approval[3] – this means submitting all your plans to the building control department. These will include:

1. architect's drawings
2. engineer's drawings
3. any other information – e.g. energy assessments.

Two: apply for a building notice[4] – this is a way of starting on site more quickly without having to submit plans to building control. If you decide to do this, you must be completely sure your builder knows the work done will comply fully with all building regulations, otherwise you may end up having to re-do bits, which would be extra time and expense.

There are private companies of approved building inspectors that can do this for you and complete the ongoing inspections as the work progresses. The benefit is that they may be more responsive than the council inspectors are able to be, although in our experience the latter works just as well as long as your builder has a good relationship with the local authority inspectors.

I don't think we were ever held up by the need for a visit. Our builder knew the building inspector well, so could call up and make arrangements directly. I guess he was also thinking ahead and getting the visit booked in ahead of time.

There are specific times when the building inspector needs to visit, including, but not limited to:

- when the foundations are poured
- before the wiring and pipework are covered up
- when the soakaway and drains are exposed.

Your builder must know exactly what the inspector needs to see and make sure they are informed in time. If they attend too late and the relevant work is covered, you may be left removing plaster when this is the last thing you want to do – never mind the expense of doing a job twice.

If you are doing a self-build with borrowed money, you may find that payments are linked to inspection points. This means you need to get through each stage to collect your next tranche of money.

New regulations

Always make sure you or your builder are up to date with new building regulations because they are updated periodically. As time goes on (we hope) they will become even more focused on aspects relating to the environment, although if you are doing an eco renovation/retrofit, you'll be doing all that anyway.

One example is the size of windows that are allowed. We all watch those marvellous builds on *Grand Designs* with envy – or, at least, I do – but the sheer scale of windows installed may soon be a thing of the past. So much heat is lost through glazing that limits are put on how much you can design in. Unless, of course, you go for top-quality triple glazing and then you might be in with a chance.

MANAGING THE PLANNING PROCESS

First stop is to go to the local council website and see what you can find out about the rules and regulations in your area.

- Talk to your architect about how much they'll do for you and how good their relationships are with the planning office.
- Talk to the planning officer yourself to get to know them and find out what the problems might be with your plans.
- Go to the web pages for planning permission and put in your postcode. This will bring up applications near you so you can see what others have done and what information/paperwork they needed to provide – e.g. reports from daylight specialists.

MANAGING YOUR NEIGHBOURS

It's tough for neighbours when building work is going on. I well remember our house shaking when the hammer drill was being used next door, so I felt huge sympathy for them when it was our turn to make a racket. It was bad enough for us and we stood to gain. They had to take the inconvenience and noise with nothing to show for it. So it's a very good idea to include your neighbours from the outset so they aren't taken unawares.

The planning stage is also the point where neighbours might get upset or anxious about your plans, so the more you've included them and helped them understand what's about to happen, the less chance they'll try to raise objections.

PARTY WALL AGREEMENT

One issue that you might well come across with your neighbours is the party wall agreement. This is relevant if you share a wall with your neighbour and that wall is going to be involved in the building work. This generally comes later on in the process because once it's signed, it only lasts for one year. So rather than have to do it again if there are delays, it is generally addressed when it's needed.

It is a paper exercise and provides the opportunity to work out some agreements with your neighbour:

- what hours the builders will be on site
- whether the builders will need access to your neighbour's property
- a record of the existing condition of the wall for comparison should any unexpected damage occur
- an opportunity for your neighbour to see the foundation plans and express any concerns about risks to the joint wall.

This is something you can do yourself and there are forms online[5] to help you. You can find a full breakdown of the law and the process on the government website.

You will also need to get a party wall agreement signed if you are building on or near the boundary with your neighbour's land – even if you are not going to be touching a building belonging to them. Do a bit of research and double check whether the Party Wall Act[6](1996) will apply to the works you are proposing.

The main issue with a party wall agreement will be the relationship you have with your neighbour. If it's good already, you've probably told them about the work you're having done and explained how much noise and disturbance there will be for them. If you don't yet have a relationship or it's been a bit testy recently, then this is the time to do something about it and this might be the perfect opportunity. But that's another book altogether!

If your situation is not straightforward, or you feel you cannot make the agreement yourself, you can appoint a party wall surveyor. These are specialists who will make sure everything is done correctly and mediate between you and your neighbour if necessary.

ENERGY PERFORMANCE CERTIFICATE

The Energy Performance Certificate (EPC) is not part of the formal planning process, but it is a formality that it's best to get on top of from the outset.

We are used to seeing energy ratings – they are part of the decision on every appliance we buy (see chapter 13), and they tell us how much energy the washing machine, dishwasher or oven we're choosing will use.

The house version of this energy rating is the Energy Performance Certificate and it's becoming increasingly important, not only because of the climate emergency and increasing energy costs, but also because it is now part of any house sale or purchase. Increasingly home buyers will want to know that the house is well insulated, warm and cheap to run. Research[7] shows that the EPC can positively affect the value of your home by up to 14% – great news for the environment.

How does the EPC work?

The EPC sets out the energy efficiency of a property on a traffic-light system (see the front cover of this book) rating from A to G. The report indicates how much the property will cost to run from an energy perspective and includes ideas for further energy-efficient improvements.

You need an accredited domestic energy assessor to do the survey for you. You can find a register online[8]. The fee for the assessment will depend on the size of your property, so clarify that when you make an appointment.

The assessor will complete a visual inspection of your house. They'll take measurements, photographs and take away information about:

- size and construction of the property
- insulation – loft, external walls and floors
- type of heating – radiators, thermostatic values, heat control thermostats, log/coal fires
- water heating
- quality and age of glazing – double or triple
- number of lights and energy-efficient lightbulbs
- effectiveness of ventilation
- solar/photovoltaic energy.

The assessor will ask about additional work you have done, whether you have any heat recovery technology, cavity wall insulation…

The calculation compares the carbon emissions of the building with a reference building of the same size, structure and usage. It will include suggestions for how you can improve your reading, such as:

- installing a more efficient heating boiler
- installing cavity wall and loft insulation
- considering energy-efficient glazing
- draught-proofing windows and doors
- installing low-energy lightbulbs
- insulating pipes and tanks
- reducing water usage
- considering renewable energy technology like wind turbines, wood-fuelled heaters and solar panels.

Given the climate emergency, I think we can assume the EPC is going to increase in importance. Already an energy reading of F or G can see mortgage applications turned down. So ensuring a strong EPC will make your house more saleable.

Your EPC assessor

Given you've got this far in the book, it's likely that you're going for some level of eco in your renovation/retrofit, in which case getting a good EPC reading will be just one more indicator that you're making the difference you want to make. All of the factors in the list opposite are included in other chapters so you have a good starting point for an exceptional EPC.

———

Who thought an EPC could be so exciting!

We wanted to know where we stood at the outset, so arranged for a visit from a recommended EPC assessor. Gian arrived on one of those days – cold and windy, builders everywhere, noise, dust; just another normal day in the life of a retrofitter. His memory is of a building site and when I look at it through his eyes, I wonder how on earth we managed to live in the place.

He did his best with all the measurements. At the time, not understanding how the process worked, we kept trying to tell him about all the changes we were going to make, thinking that would improve the reading. Once he'd told us a few times that he couldn't count anything that wasn't in place, we shut up and accepted that this was just the starting point.

Now the work is mostly completed, we asked him back to reassess. It was a lovely visit – seeing the reaction of someone who was there in the worst of it is such a delight – and he was as excited as we were to find out what the new rating would be.

Gian gave us an excellent piece of advice that I pass on to you – involve your EPC assessor from the outset. We sort of did that, but we could have invited him back at significant stages as well. The downside of a retrofit is that most of your hard work will never be seen – it's all hidden behind the décor. And quite rightly, but it's then harder for the assessor to fully understand what you've done. So talk with them, find out how often they should come and when would be the best times for a visit – e.g. before the wall / floor insulation is covered up. They can become a real support in the process, making suggestions while you have time to adapt.

———

Materials you need for your assessment

Keep in mind that the EPC assessment is entirely evidence-based, so nothing can be included until it is fully installed and in use. Everything you have done needs to be supported by certification or signed letters from installers. So take some time to gather the information your EPC assessor will need:

- Signed statement about insulation – if you don't have an interim EPC visit, ask your builder to sign a written statement about the type and depth of insulation that has been installed in the floors and external walls.
- If you've installed solar panels, the document that shows the quality and kilowatt hours the panels will produce.

- The FENSA (guarantee) document for your double or triple-glazed windows.
- Documents about your heating system and boiler – ASHP or gas condensing boiler.

We had also gathered together all the photos taken along the way, but these are actually of no help – they can't be relied on in such an evidence-based process. Only the pictures taken by the assessor at the time are valid (hence the suggestion about interim visits).

You'll need to arrange access to the whole house (so make the bed!), including the loft, so everything that can be seen, is seen. We did OK with this (I had made the bed!) , although with a bit of advance thinking we could have made it easier to see the insulation in the loft. So thinking it through beforehand will make the whole visit easier.

Don't expect to get a result on the spot. Once the visit is complete, the assessor takes all the information away to input into software that then produces your EPC rating. This will be sent to you a few days after your visit together with any recommendations for additional action.

Newsflash: our EPC went from a D to a B, which is the norm for a new house. Pretty good going! And the only other recommendation they could make was to put in a solar water heating unit. There are some elements of retrofitting an eco house that have yet to be included in the EPC calculations but hopefully it will all be upgraded soon. So when your time comes, you may be set for an A.

SUMMARY

- Permitted development requires no permission, but you need to check carefully against your plans. You can get a legal Lawful Development Certificate if you wish. Some types of permitted development, such as extensions over a certain size, may need prior approval.

- Planning permission is required if your build will have an impact on the outside of the house. Ideally it will take eight weeks for the council to decide the application once it has been validated. Depending on the resources the council has available, it may take longer to validate the application.

- If your plans don't fit requirements, you may be able to amend them and resubmit to the planning office. Your architect will help with the whole process.

- You will also have to comply with building regulations, which cover the structural and safety aspects of the build.

- You can make a full plans application or apply for a building notice, which gets you on site sooner. With the latter, you must make sure you comply fully with all building regulations or you may have to undo some of your work.

- Include your neighbours wherever you can. They have to put up with the inconvenience as well as you, but they have nothing to gain.

- If you will be working on or up to the property boundary, you need to get a party wall agreement signed by your neighbour.

- Invite your EPC assessor to visit periodically through the building process, so they can see the details of what you do for themselves. It will help them be more accurate.

- Get an initial reading of your EPC just for the pleasure of seeing it improve when it's all finished.

PLANNING AND BUILDING CONTROL

1. http://www.gov.uk/government/publications/permitted-development-rights-for-householders-technical-guidance
2. http://www.gov.uk/appeal-planning-decision
3. https://www.planningportal.co.uk/applications/building-control-applications/building-control/how-to-get-approval/pre-site-approval/full-plans
4. https://www.planningportal.co.uk/applications/building-control-applications/building-control/how-to-get-approval/pre-site-approval/building-notice
5. https://www.gov.uk/government/publications/preventing-and-resolving-disputes-in-relation-to-party-walls/the-party-wall-etc-act-1996-explanatory-booklet
6. https://www.gov.uk/government/publications/preventing-and-resolving-disputes-in-relation-to-party-walls/the-party-wall-etc-act-1996-explanatory-booklet
7. https://www.moneysupermarket.com/gas-and-electricity/value-of-efficiency/
8. http://www.gov.uk/find-energy-certificate

CHAPTER 7
INSULATION

I f you'd told me two years ago that I'd be utterly fascinated by insulation, I'd have been very confused – who me? Now I can't think of anything more exciting to talk about.

Insulation is the baseline for an eco home of any sort. The task is to create heat in the most environmentally friendly way possible, then hold onto it – and insulation is a key part of making this possible.

There are three main areas that need insulation:

1. external walls
2. ground floor
3. roof.

Each will make a real difference to the warmth in your house and the amount of energy you use. If you can do all three, then even better.

Important: it's not possible to address insulation on its own – you have to address it in conjunction with **breathability, airtightness and ventilation**. All these elements are directly linked, so read those chapters alongside this one. Understanding the inter-relationship from the outset will help you to ask the pertinent questions at the right time.

There are three terms to understand before exploring your options in terms of insulation:

- airtightness
- thermal bridge
- U values.

AIRTIGHTNESS

Let's start with airtightness. John and I made the assumption that insulation would create a cosy layer to keep the house warm and be key to cutting out the many draughts that plague old houses such as ours. Sadly this is only half true. No matter how tightly insulation materials are fitted together, some air will come through unless everything is sealed up. (See chapter 8.)

In our front room we spent hours putting in the underfloor insulation (described below). We then laid the original floorboards back over the top in preparation for that wonderful day when the new carpet would go down. Fortunately I was able to arrange an airtightness test before that happened and we discovered that despite our best efforts there were draughts coming up between the floor boards. It was a very depressing moment, but a good lesson in understanding how airtightness and insulation work together.

THERMAL BRIDGE

This brings us neatly onto thermal bridges. You'll hear the phrase bandied around a lot and it can take a while to work out what builders and architects are referring to.

A **thermal bridge**, also called a **cold bridge**, **heat bridge** or **thermal bypass**, is an area that conducts heat more easily than the surrounding materials. This means that overall it will lose more heat than would be expected and need more heat to keep the space warm. It may also cause condensation as warm air hits the cold surface/thermal bridge. So take really good care of these areas when insulating.

Reasons for a thermal bridge are:

- a break in insulation
- less insulation than the surrounding area
- an exposed metal surface without insulation.

A good example was lagging the water pipes in our kitchen. Pipe insulation materials had been put around the front of the warm pipes, which gave some protection, but not at the back where they butted up against the cold wall. This meant there was a cold bridge unprotected by a warm material.

Another place was along the steel that holds up the original end of the house. We had been very concerned that there wasn't enough insulation along the steel, leaving a cold surface underneath the plaster that would draw the warm air away. We were able to check it out with a thermal imaging camera (see below) and found that it was nice and warm, so not a thermal bridge after all.

UNDERSTANDING U VALUES

The U value tells you how effective your insulation will be. It measures the heat lost through a given thickness of a material or a composite element, such as a wall. You don't need to know how it's calculated or have an in-depth knowledge. All you need to understand is that lower is better. Once you know that, you can determine whether the material of your choice will give the results you're looking for.

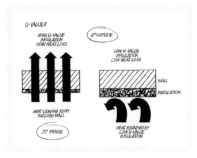

The lower the U value of insulation, the more warmth in the room

The measure of U value is watts per metre squared – W/m^2K. The K refers to a kelvin, which is a base unit of temperature. To give you some figures for comparison, the U values required by current building regulations for a new build are:

- external walls / floors - 0.18
- W/m^2K roof - 0.15 W/m^2K
- windows - 0.14 W/m^2K.

To put this into perspective:

- An uninsulated 225mm solid brick wall will have a U value of 2.7 W/m^2K.
- Add 120mm of wood fibre insulation and this comes down to 0.29 W/m^2K.

This is why it's worth insulating wherever you can. If you find you need to understand in more depth, you can read about it online.

R value – this is the other measure that comes up when researching insulation. In fact U value and R value are just the inverse of each other. Whereas U value measures the rate of heat transfer, R value measures the ability of the material to block heat transfer. So as the R value goes up, the U value goes down. Please don't ask me why there are two measures saying roughly the same thing, but I do suggest looking into it further when it's relevant to your choices.

TYPES OF INSULATION

The exact amount of insulation needed to achieve a lower U value will depend on the material you use. There are a number of options to choose from, with the main point of difference being method of manufacture and the impact this has on the environment.

The most commonly used insulation is not the most environmentally friendly, so this is the moment to refer to your touchstone. Once you are clear on your priorities – environment or budget – you can review the options available in your chosen area.

Environmentally friendly materials

The most commonly used environmentally friendly material[1] is made from wood fibre. It's a robust and flexible insulation that can be used for floors, roofs and walls. It is recyclable, locks in carbon as it grows and is relatively free of pollutants. It also has low U values plus it's 100% compostable and recyclable at the end of its life. This is always a major question for me – will it rot down at the end of the day? If it won't then however good it is now, it's going to cost the earth in the end.

Wood fibre comes in soft batts (long rectangles of compacted fibre) – or hard board (like traditional plasterboard). It can be used in a range of settings – under suspended floors, on walls and in the roof. Because the material is flexible, it can be packed into tight spaces to cut down on draughts.

There are other benefits to wood fibre. It gives high levels of noise insulation, so if you have noisy neighbours (or you are noisy neighbours) it will work well on adjoining walls, having 6 to 12 times the density of synthetic options. It also gives an added level of fire safety and reduces humidity so helps to prevent dampness.

There are other environmental options. Sheep's wool is a good one because sheep need to be sheared at least once a year and the fleeces often go to waste. There is the argument that encouraging meat production is bad for the earth, which is well proven. However, if it is being produced then it may make sense to use the 'waste' materials. And because it is organic, the wool will rot down at the end of its life.

Other options are cork, straw, hemp and jute – there is even insulation made from old denim jeans. So there is no shortage of options; it just takes some time to go exploring and researching to make sure you know what you are doing.

Sort of environmentally friendly

Another insulation material that can be used is **mineral wool**[2] – rock, stone or glass wool. It is made from molten rock combined with a binder and a small amount of oil and is exposed to very high temperatures during production making it highly non-flammable.

In terms of the environment, mineral wool isn't as friendly as natural materials, but it's much better than oil-based synthetics. It is also less expensive than natural materials, so could be a good choice if you're concerned about both environment and budget. It comes in soft batts or hard boards, similar to wood fibre, so can be used in all the same situations: roof spaces, walls and suspended floors. It can also be tightly packed to reduce draughts and is both non-combustible and resistant to rot.

The biggest downside of mineral wool is that the main material needs to be quarried. Also, if it gets wet the thermal conductivity is increased so it becomes less efficient. And a lot of energy is required to produce it.

Not environmentally friendly

PIR is the most commonly used insulation board. You'll recognise PIR by the silver 'tin foil'-style coating on the outside and you'll see it on most building sites. PIR is made from petrochemical substances, so not well liked by those with an eye to the earth. Its production releases emissions into the air and water, as well as creating hazardous waste, and it has high embodied energy – i.e. it takes a lot of energy to produce it.

It is also very important to note that, should the material catch fire, higher levels of toxic gas will be produced than with other insulation materials and it is considered a real danger to health and environment.

If budget is a big issue, then PIR is cheaper than other options and it is easily available. It can be used in a house with cavity walls, but its lack of breathability makes it a poor match for old solid wall breathable constructions (See chapter 9). It is OK for walls, but its rigidity makes it less efficient in lofts and under suspended floors, because it can't be packed closely together and it may shift over time, producing gaps for draughts to come through.

Which material to use

In terms of choices, the first and most important thing is to insulate. This will make a real difference to your comfort, your bills, your carbon footprint and the next generation.

If your budget is limited and your only option is to use PIR, that's better than not insulating at all. However, if you can also use environmentally friendly materials, you will do even more for the earth, so your carbon footprint and the kids will thank you in the long run.

INSULATING WALLS

Because environment is important to us, John and I asked our architect to keep this in mind when designing the extension. His recommendation was to:

1. put a breathable membrane across the wall
2. build a stud frame to hold the insulation
3. put 80mm of wood fibre insulation batts (in our case, Pavaflex) into each gap in the framework
4. cover with rigid 40mm boards of Isolair (the wood fibre equivalent of plasterboard).

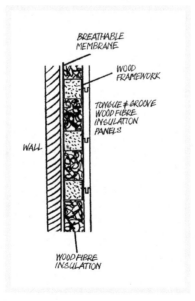

Insulation of a sold brick wall with eco friendly wood fibre batts

Altogether this gave us 120mm of insulation, which makes the house feel very cosy indeed. (As a small spin-off, it also provides lovely deep window sills for plants!) We decided to stick with this process as we worked our way back through the house.

We found out about Pavatex products by speaking with the technical people at Ecological Building Systems[3] and Unity Lime[4]. They were very helpful and remarkably balanced in their views. We got to know their experts pretty well by the time we'd finished.

If you do decide to go with PIR, it can be attached directly to the wall with either an adhesive or insulation anchors (screws with a big circular plastic head). By the way, if you have any issues with penetrating damp, make sure these are dealt with before putting in any insulation, but particularly if using non-breathable PIR, otherwise it will only make the damp worse and the moisture will downgrade the insulation.

Quality control

Once the materials were chosen and the wood frame for the insulation constructed, inserting the Pavaflex was something we could do ourselves. Cutting the batts requires a saw but is very light work and the wooden frame holds them safely in place. It does require a sense of perfection, because each gap or missed angle means more draughts and cold spots, so it was important to get it right. We became adept at putting the jigsaw together and stuffing each gap with little bits of the wood fibre.

If your builders are not familiar with the material or you really want to be sure it's done well, it is worth keeping an eye out at this point. You can easily make good on your own and half an hour stuffing gaps can be really satisfying at the end of a long and dusty day.

Plastering – the final layer

Since wood fibre is a breathable material, it needs to be covered with lime plaster, which is also breathable (see chapter 9). It doesn't look very different from regular plaster – just slightly more rustic in finish. The downside is that it takes a number of coats to complete, with drying time in between, so it is a longer job overall. As long as this is scheduled into the programme it's not a problem. Once finished it behaves as ordinary plaster in all but one area – the paint you use must also be breathable (see chapter 14).

It can be tricky to find a lime plasterer, however. If anyone reading this is looking for a new profession or specialism, this could be just the thing. There are specialists out there, but they tend to focus on proper old listed buildings, not just slightly old Victorian; and big renovations, rather than small ones like ours. Demand is sure to increase, so there will soon be a regular flow of work looking for a provider.

––––––

Anyone know a lime plasterer?

I had no idea there were different kinds of plaster until some wise soul thought to tell us we needed lime plaster on our breathable insulation. Our first reaction was to get onto the web and go looking for someone to help us. Only when the pages came up blank did we begin to suspect what was to come.

Lime is always needed in really old houses – stately homes, Shakespearian cottages, you know the sort of thing. It's sexy, interesting work that takes months at a time. Enter the owner of a 'young' Victorian terrace with just a few walls that need doing and the level of interest drops over a cliff.

We were right up against the wire with the arrival of the kitchen looming and running out of time for the lime to be applied and dry. Christmas was on the horizon, so there was little sun or warmth to rely on and we were getting desperate. And I was so fed up of cooking in a building yard; I really wanted us to move on.

We finally sorted it with the help of our kitchen provider. Someone's son had a friend who did lime and he was willing to take us on. It went well and, because lime takes longer, Matthew soon felt like a family member. So if you're on for the environmental approach, start looking from the outset − this definitely isn't one to get caught out on.

———

Insulating cavity walls

Houses built from 1920 onwards are likely to be built with cavity walls. This is a double skin of bricks with a gap in between, designed to prevent problems with damp. The cavity stops moisture from the outside entering the inside of a building, and helps the water drain back out of the wall again.

If your house was built after 1970, there is a chance that the cavity will automatically have been filled with insulation. If it was built in the 1990s or later, this was compulsory. However, it is important to keep an eye on it, because some types of insulation will settle or DIY work may create holes that disturb the materials, creating cold bridges.

Polystyrene balls (EPS) have been used to fill cavity walls in recent years. It is a better insulator than anything else with a low U value, so is a good choice from that perspective. It will also tell you straight away if the cavity is breached by DIY work, because balls dribble out of the wall!

The downside to EPS is that it comes from oil and goes through a long process in production, so has high embodied energy. It won't biodegrade, so your insulation may well outlive your house by a few hundred years.

Wood fibre can be blown into the cavity as a good environmental option.

NB: spray foam – some companies may recommend using a spray foam. If you are considering this, please look into it very carefully. There are a number of reasons to be wary:

- there is a risk of toxic fumes being given off both immediately and, in some cases, long term
- the foam can trap dampness, which can then lead to mould and rot, so unless you are completely certain you can keep it dry it's worth looking into different options
- once installed, you can't remove it, so if you find it is causing a moisture problem, for example, you might need to replace the entire floor/roof/wall structure
- because of this mortgage and insurance companies don't like it. This is especially true in lofts, where it gets stuck around the roof timbers and causes problems
- Spray foam cannot be recycled in any way so is a long term risk to the environment.

If this is suggested to you, please look into it very carefully and make sure you understand[5] all the risks.

Interesting fact: if you live in a terraced house with cavity walls, make sure you insulate the adjoining wall. Where the party wall is an uninsulated cavity wall it can create a thermal bypass effect, which means that the cavity acts like a chimney and carries heat out of the house.

If you need to insulate for acoustics, remember that natural materials have much better acoustic qualities so you'll get the best results with wood fibre.

Insulating irregular walls – discovering Diathonite

There are always going to be occasions when the shape of the wall or design of the space won't allow for a wood frame system – which was exactly the situation with the traditional Victorian bay window in our front room.

To put the same depth of insulation around the window would have impacted the room size and would have been very complex given the shape of the bay. It was a challenge for a long time. In moments of frustration we even discussed not doing that room at all. Fortunately my perfectionist side kicked in and I went on the hunt for a solution. It had to be possible.

After long, unproductive discussions with every professional we could think of, I took a punt and wrote to Clare Nash[6], an architect in Oxford. She had given a talk to Sustainable St Albans[7] so I knew she was a keen environmentalist. Clare generously responded to my rather desperate email and told me about Diathonite[8] – a thermal plaster that copes well with corners and angles.

The beauty of Diathonite is that it can easily vary in thickness, so we could have maximum thickness on flat walls and reduce the thickness where necessary to maintain the corners of the bay. The biggest problem was finding the right expert – it is usually applied by lime plasterers!

The first step was to remove the old lime plaster and get back to the bare brick. The original coving also had to be removed, so we found a specialist to make a template before it came down. The final pre-work was to build a deeper frame to the bay window to accommodate the increased depth of wall once the Diathonite was in place.

The specialist plasterers trowelled on the Diathonite in three layers, which meant there was no problem with shading the thickness in different areas. It took a few days of waiting for each layer to dry before the next one could be applied. Finally they put a fine skim of finishing lime plaster to give a smooth surface. You can read an interesting, more detailed account in this blog from Green Building Store[9].

We are delighted with the result. Our desire to retain the bay window did cost us something in thermal efficiency. This was no fault of Diathonite – it was our choice to reduce the thickness to retain the shape. So although most of the walls have a thickness of 60mm, around the window it is down to 40mm.

External insulation – sometimes it is easier to insulate the outside of a property to avoid internal disruption and loss of space in your rooms. The choice of insulation material is the same as for inside: wood fibre, mineral wool or PIR. One other possibility is an insulating render.

The usual method is to fix rigid boards to the wall – tongue and groove, to prevent any gaps – or to use insulating render such as cork. Diathonite can also be used externally.

If you're considering external wall insulation, it's worth taking time to research on line for information[10] before going ahead. This clearly isn't totally straightforward, so make sure you find out as much as you can about it before reaching your decision.

INSULATING FLOORS

Cutting out the cold from beneath the floor (the sub-floor void) has been a game changer in our house. I know the prospect of moving all the furniture and getting in among the floorboards is daunting, but I guarantee it will be worth it. So please do include this in your plans for home insulation.

How you go about it will depend on the type of floor you are dealing with.

Concrete floors

In the new extension we have a concrete block and beam floor. By its nature, concrete is freezing so must be insulated to reduce cold coming up from the floor and to stop it leaching heat from the house. This is a standard construction method:

- the concrete/block and beam is laid and allowed to dry
- rigid insulation is laid on top to form a barrier between the cold of the concrete and the room and heat of pipes
- underfloor heating pipes (if you are having them) are laid on top of the insulation
- a screed is put on top of the insulation/pipes to protect them and to provide a smooth, flat surface for the floor.

Given the need for a thin, rigid insulation, we did in fact go for 100mm of PIR here – in this case, Kingspan. We later discovered that Passivhaus recommends 200mm, so we could have done more - as long as we'd sorted out floor levels ahead of time.

If you have an old house, you may have a concrete floor that sits directly onto the compacted earth with no void underneath. This needs a conversation with your builder or architect about the best way to insulate and how to manage the question of damp – depending on whether there is a damp-proof membrane (DPM) or a damp-proof course (DPC) and if so, how they work together. If all else fails, putting down a good thick rug with a rubber underlay will help keep the heat in the room. Make sure the rug fits right up to the wall to reduce cold and draughts.

Suspended wood floors

Suspended floors are common in any house built before the 1960s so we have them in all the original parts of our 1901 house.

The walls of our house are built on very shallow foundations that are just slightly wider than the thickness of the walls themselves. In between walls, underneath the joists and floor-boards, is basic earth. Slightly alarming when I first saw it, I must say.

Wooden joists run between the walls and, when covered with floorboards, they form the floor we walk on. The cavity beneath the floor – the sub-floor void – needs continuous air flow to avoid damp and condensation, hence the presence of air bricks, which must never be blocked up. This is great for the health of the building, but desperate in terms of draughts coming up through the floor and making rooms cold.

So adding insulation is a must and now we've done it, I think it might be one of the most significant alterations we made. No more cold feet when watching TV at night and no more rampant draughts rushing through the house.

The conventional way would be for the builder to fix PIR between the joists. There is plenty of literature and YouTube videos on how to do this, if you want to do it yourself. However, PIR really isn't the best option for a suspended floor. In any floor there will be movement and with old houses in particular the gaps between the joists are unlikely to be even. The rigidity of PIR means it can't mould itself to the space.

Also, as time goes by it will settle, leaving gaps in the insulation.

Given that our priority was to be eco, we continued with our plan to use wood fibre batts. This turned out also to be the best option for floors because it is highly flexible and can be stuffed into the space really tightly to block any gaps.

We decided to do this part of the job ourselves. This was partly out of a need to make sure it was done really thoroughly and to save some money, but also because we felt ready to get our hands dirty – for the first hour, anyway! The level of underfloor insulation we wanted was going beyond what our builders expected – we were going for high level cosy. When it's your own toes getting cold, you're more prepared to go above and beyond to get it right.

The task was to fill each gap between joists with wood fibre – in our case, two 80mm Pavaflex batts one on top of the other. But how to do it was a bit of a puzzle – we obviously couldn't sit the batts directly on the earth , because that would block the air bricks. We couldn't find any literature or videos to guide us so we had to get inventive. Fortunately this is one area where John came up with the right way all on his own, as we later discovered when we read about the same approach in an Ecological Building Systems blog[11].

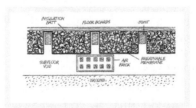

Insulation under a suspended floor, avoiding the air bricks

1. We created a holder/cradle for the Pavaflex batts between each joist by stapling a continuous

waterproof, breathable roofing membrane to both sides with sufficient slack to hold the insulation. **NB:** it's very important to run a continuous layer to minimise draughts coming through any joins. Where we were unable to do this, we made sure the join was sealed before replacing the floorboards.

2. We went for two 80mm batts per space, giving us a total of 160mm insulation throughout the underfloor space. Given the need for air flow in the sub-floor void, we had to take great care not to block the air bricks. Their job is to keep air flowing to avoid damp and condensation so we positioned the bottom of the cradle just above the top of the air bricks.

3. We measured each gap individually because the spaces between the joists were always different and we cut each batt to the correct size. The density of the batt is such that it is very easy to cut with a saw on a table surface.

4. We cut each batt slightly bigger than needed so that it had to be pushed into place, aimed at reducing any draughts coming up from the sub-floor void. It is also recommended to position the batts so they are 10mm taller than the joists to create more of an airtight seal when the floorboards go back down.

5. Then we covered the whole construction with another layer of the breathable membrane to combat any remaining draughts (see chapter 8). This went on top of the joists and insulation batts and all the overlaps of the membrane are sealed together.

6. We sealed up the junction between the wall and the floor throughout. For this we used Contega[12], a very sticky indoor sealing tape that stops air emerging through the wall–floor junction.

7. We then replaced the floorboards, squashing down the membrane and the extra 10mm of insulation to create an even better airtight seal.

I have since discovered that just 100mm of insulation under a suspended floor can reduce heat loss by 65% – so it was a job worth doing.

———

Where's your lorry parked?

We had a moment of panic when insulating under the dining room floor. The next big job on the list was the underfloor heating (UFH) and pinning down a date had been like knitting fog. When the plumbers suddenly said they would be with us the next day, we realised we'd have to burn the midnight oil – we couldn't bear to put them off. But... we didn't have enough batts to finish the job and the building merchants would have to order it in. You can imagine the expletives – they heated the house up all on their own!

We decided that John would start with what we did have, while I drove to Northampton to pick up as much Pavaflex as I could get in the car. So that dark and stormy night (and I really mean stormy) I found myself searching for a large builders' yard just off the M1. The person behind the desk was remarkably helpful given that it was nearly closing time and I was in a bit of a flap. But my spirits lifted when she asked me where I'd parked my lorry. Clearly I wasn't at my most elegant – the combined effects of living in a building site and covid – but none of that mattered when she thought I might be someone who could drive a lorry. Go me!

Needless to say, I got myself and the batts home – pretty hairy at times, but we made it. And, of course, the plumbers changed their schedule so it was all in vain, but it was done and I looked like someone who might drive a lorry. Made my month!

———

INSULATING LOFTS

A nugget of the physics I remember from school is that hot air rises, meaning every bit of energy you put into your house is heading for the loft and straight out through the roof. So adding in a layer of warm, cosy insulating material there has to be an important job.

This is an area of insulation that we're all familiar with and there are still government schemes in the UK giving a subsidy[13] to help with the cost of doing the work. If you're not in the UK, go to your equivalent site and hopefully there will be something there to help you.

In wintertime the easy way to check the effectiveness of your loft insulation is to see how long it takes for your roof to clear on a frosty morning. Unless there is very strong sunlight – in which case all the other nearby roofs will clear at the same rate – any melting will be caused by heat coming up through the roof tiles. A well-insulated roof will hang onto frost for a long time.

As with underfloor insulation, using a flexible material is a must. PIR does not work well, because it shifts and settles, leaving gaps in the covering.

The options here are the same as for underneath the floor:

- wood fibre, sheep's wool, hemp etc – low U value, sustainable and effective
- mineral wool: rock or stone – reasonably sustainable and low U value

How you go about insulating the loft will depend on how you use it:

1. an empty loft space
2. a loft space that is used for storage
3. a loft space that is used as a room.

An empty loft space

When your loft is an empty space, insulating is straightforward. Your task is to line the floor of the loft with maximum warmth to stop heat from the working house being lost into the vacant space.

The recommended minimum thickness for insulation material is 270mm. This has increased from just 25mm in the 1980s, so it's good to see we are achieving some change on behalf of the environment.

You are looking for a U value for the whole roof of 0.15 in a renovation or extension, so the exact thickness needed will depend on which material you choose to use.

The ideal approach is to put a layer between the ceiling joists, then cover it with subsequent layers at right angles. This will prevent any thermal bridges and unwanted heat loss – as long as you also seal up the joins between the insulation material.

There is one exception to loft coverage – be careful not to put insulation underneath the water tank. This is the one place you actually want a thermal bridge, so that warm air penetrating from the house to the tank stops the water freezing. You can still put it on top of the tank to reduce heat loss.

Clearly 270mm (10+ inches for those who still visualise on the old system) is a huge amount and rises well above the level of the joists. So this is only possible when the loft space is not being used.

It's also important to improve airtightness/vapour control at ceiling level as well as insulating, and to increase ventilation to the roof space if you can. When you increase the insulation at ceiling level you create a steeper temperature gradient between the warm room below and the cold loft above. This means that any water vapour that gets into the loft space is much more likely to condense in the loft and create perfect conditions for mould growth. Creating an airtightness layer (see chapter 8) will reduce the risk of such unintended consequences.

You don't necessarily need to introduce a membrane to do this; just be sure to seal up any cracks in the ceiling, and the junction between the ceiling and the top of the wall. Also watch out for any pipework that might penetrate the ceiling and seal around this.

When you want to use the loft for storage

If you want to use your loft for storage, you need to do it without compressing the insulation material because this reduces energy efficiency.[14] Like a duvet on your bed, it's the thickness of the material and the air it holds that keeps your house warm so anything that reduces that thickness will cost you in lost heat.

To achieve this without squashing all the warm air out of your insulation material, you can put in a system of supports – loft legs – that hold a floor above the level of the insulation. The supports are set in place as the insulation goes down, then the boarding is laid on top. This prevents you touching the insulation when you get something out of the loft (more of an issue with synthetic fibres) and stops any air being forced from the insulation by compression.

When the loft is also a room

If the loft is also a room then the insulation must go between and below the rafters, stopping hot air leaving through the roof tiles and cold air coming back in the same way. Because the building regulations require a U value of 0.15, we're talking about a similar thickness of insulation material applied between the ceiling rafters – i.e. 270mm. This means you reduce the head height considerably. Best to consult a loft conversion expert to do this work. You will find ideas for how to go about it online.

If the room is already completed and you're concerned about the effectiveness of the insulation, there is the option to line the ceiling with a wooden structure and a thick layer of insulation. Of course, this needs a ceiling high enough so you can still stand up in the space.

In our case, the central part of the loft space has been made into a useable room, with the eaves serving as storage space, so we needed a combination of approaches. We have a cantilevered staircase so it can't be used as a bedroom, but it has provided a great office space for home working over the years. We're not quite ready to close it up for good, so had to think about insulating both the floor and the roof.

In the eaves space, we used sheep's wool of 100mm thickness with wooden board underneath. This allowed us to continue with storage, but didn't give the full quality of insulation needed. So we also insulated between and below the rafters using 50mm Pavatherm and 40mm Isolair to make up the difference. We continued the same process in the living space.

Dealing with the floor reduced the loss of warm air coming up from the house, and lining the ceiling of the room blocked any heating in the office space from flying away through the roof. It has also stopped condensation dripping from the cold roofing felt under the tiles as it was doing previously.

If you're going the whole hog and retiling your roof, the best option is to put insulation above the rafters, to create a 'warm roof'. This is often done in new houses and will give the best results.

Please note: when putting insulation between the rafters, take care to keep it in line with the tops of the rafters. There needs to be a ventilation gap above the rafters and you don't want to block this airflow.

Inside the loft

We didn't do this work ourselves – I can't think of anything worse; bent double in an enclosed space wasn't my idea of an interesting time! Plus the fact that insulating the loft had become a thorny subject. Not only was it a challenging task – strange shapes, low head height, hot or very cold – there was the question of all the stuff accumulated over the 40 years we've lived in the house. And the equally thorny fact that one of us is a hoarder and one is a thrower. With all the change in the house, this was just a step too far, so it was the last thing to happen.

Every sentimental school painting, Father's Day card, cuddly toy was there – you name it, we had it. On days when we felt strong we'd started weeding, returning large bin bags of stuff to each of our girls to do with as they wished. It was a great relief – for us, not them! I spent hours on Freegle (see chapter 15) and the charity shops took some of the strain.

Eventually we found someone willing to do the job, but by now it was summertime – and one of the few really hot weeks we had that summer. I felt so sorry for them up there, sweating away in a tight stuffy space. We do have a large dormer window that was wide open so at least there was some fresh air, albeit hot and steamy.

It was towards the end of the job that the workmen realised something: whereas they had been really hot, they were now very comfortable; and where it had been noisy, it was now much quieter. This was proof positive that the insulation was working – heat from the house and through the roof was so much reduced that they were cool and the play noises from a nearby school were only a faint murmur through the window. What a success!

———

Big hint – don't forget the loft hatch! It's so easy to line the floor and forget that the top of the hatch is also a bit of floor. We got caught out by this like so many others, then had to go back and put it right.

It's also important to make sure the hatch closes tightly to make it airtight. We extended the sheep's wool beyond the size of the hatch so it covered any gaps. We also added in a very tight fastener – like the fastening on a Kilner jar – to make sure the close was as efficient as possible.

THERMAL IMAGING CAMERA

At some point you might want to check on the effectiveness of your insulation and a thermal imaging camera is the ideal way to do this. Some councils have them to borrow[15], which is what we did. The only barrier to use is that you need to do it in cold weather with a well-warmed house so you have a temperature difference of at least 10* Celsius between inside and outside. Then you are on your way.

The camera is useful to find out whether the insulation in your loft, wall or floors has any gaps or if any areas have been missed. It is also very helpful if you have cavity wall insulation and you want to check if it has settled or if there are spaces where it has come out of the wall as a result of DIY.

The camera is also useful for finding a number of other issues:

- cold air coming up between the floorboards (so you can seal them more efficiently)
- radiators that are not functioning smoothly – colder at the top than the bottom or vice versa
- hot air from radiators that is leaking through the walls to the outside and shows they need insulation behind them
- windows that are really cold and need replacing or protecting by heavy curtains
- windows joins that are not fully sealed
- letterboxes that let in cold draughts.

The list goes on. It's quite an adventure taking the camera around your home. It's amazing what you can find out. It's not complex to use – just needs a bit of time to understand then you can get full value for your allocated time.

We used pictures from the camera to engage with the company that put in our triple-glazed kitchen doors. The triple-glazed units were doing fine, but the camera showed us that there were cold gaps where the door frame met the wall. We showed the engineer the thermal images and that meant he could go straight to the problem. It turned out the latch at the top had pinged off the sash and didn't connect with the rest of the frame. Fortunately it just took a moment to put right so, together with a couple of other adjustments, he left us with much better fitting doors. Once the weather turns cold again, I'll be able to use the camera to give the doors a final check.

SUMMARY

- Insulation serves to keep the house warm − like a duvet laid on the walls, under the floor and in the roof.
- Decide whether you want to use conventional or sustainable materials.
- If using sustainable materials, the whole system will need to be breathable.
- Insulation doesn't ensure airtightness so make sure to seal up any joins, regardless of how well the insulation has been put in.
- If you have a difficult structure, a thermal plaster such as Diathonite might be a good solution.
- Start looking for a lime plasterer early on or alert your builder to the need so they can start looking.
- Remember that insulation and airtightness are different, so before you do anything, read the chapter on airtightness. (see chapter 8)

---

1. http://www.insulation-info.co.uk/eco-friendly-insulation
2. http://www.greenspec.co.uk/building-design/insulation-mineral
3. http://www.ecologicalbuildingsystems.com
4. https://unitylime.co.uk
5. http://www.homelogic.co.uk/is-spray-foam-insulation-toxic

6. https://clarenasharchitecture.co.uk/?sfw=pass1652384592
7. https://sustainablestalbans.org
8. http://www.ecologicalbuildingsystems.com/product/diathonite-thermactive
9. http://www.greenbuildingstore.co.uk/lower-royd-retrofit-internal-wall-insulation
10. http://www.homebuilding.co.uk/advice/external-wall-insulation
11. http://www.ecologicalbuildingsystems.com/post/best-practice-approach-insulating-suspended-timber-floors
12. http://www.ecologicalbuildingsystems.com/product/contega-solido-sl
13. http://www.government-grants.co.uk/home-insulation-grants/free-insulation
14. http://www.thegreenage.co.uk/loft-insulation-storage
15. https://sustainablestalbans.org/thermal-imaging

CHAPTER 8
AIRTIGHTNESS

O n this journey towards building a warm, comfortable and environmentally friendly house, we have to pay particular attention to draughts because they can leak away 20% of the heat we've worked so hard to create. The word we're looking for here is airtightness. However, as always, it's a complex story.

Important: it's not possible to address airtightness on its own; you have to address it in conjunction with **breathability, insulation and ventilation**. All these elements are directly linked, so read those chapters alongside this one. Understanding the inter-relationship from the outset will help you to ask the pertinent questions at the right time.

Airtightness is all to do with the woolly jumper effect: think about going out for a walk on a cold windy day. If you just put on a cosy jumper you'll be frozen by the time you're halfway down the road because cold air will just blow straight through the gaps in the knitting. However, put a thin windproof jacket on as well and you'll feel very warm. You need both layers – the jacket to keep the air out and the jumper to keep you warm. One won't work without the other.

According to Sofie Pelsmakers, author of *The Environmental Design Pocketbook*[1], "you can insulate as much as you like to reduce the U value of the floor, but you'll still get cold feet if you don't address airtightness." So, airtightness alongside insulation is vital for comfort and the environment.

WHAT IS AIRTIGHTNESS?

The term is pretty self-explanatory – the objective is to stop all draughts coming into your house. The solution is to be precise, detailed and nitpicky, finding every opening – large or minuscule – that will allow external air to enter the space. In essence you're creating a windproof jacket for your home, filling in every crack, sliver and cranny that might link inside to the outside and provide a passageway for cold air.

Air goes looking for entry points when there is a pressure difference between inside and outside. This happens on a daily basis courtesy of the wind. The wind blows into the side of the house and creates positive pressure that pushes air into the building. This is then matched by negative pressure inside of the house so air is sucked out. Even with a slight breeze you begin to get a pressure difference between inside and outside, which means that air – and usually carefully warmed air – is leaking out.

In addition, in winter when the heating is turned on, warm air rises, building pressure in the first floor, which in turn draws air up from the ground floor. If those ground-level floors are not airtight and insulated, cold air will come up from the sub-floor void. In other words – b****y cold!

If you want a full-blown professional explanation, try the Passivhaus Trust website[2].

Understand the lingo

Some helpful terms when it comes to talking airtightness:

- thermal envelope – your house
- thermal comfort – feeling comfortable without extra thick socks
- airtightness line – the connection between all airtight elements of the build – interconnected materials, flexible sealed joints and components of the building envelope: a constant barrier between cold and warm air.

You'll come across these terms whenever you read about the subject, but you can also persuade your builder you're serious by using the terms in the right way.

MEASURING AIRTIGHTNESS

Air leakage is measured as the rate of leakage per m^2 of external envelope (i.e. the exterior of the house) per hour at an artificial pressure differential through the envelope of 50 Pa (Pascals – a unit of pressure). This is written down as m^3/hrm^2@50Pa.

Building regulations stipulate $8m^3/hr/m^2$@50Pa, dropping to $5m^3/hr/m^2$@50Pa in 2025, which is a handy benchmark for your project. A Passivhaus will have a leakage rate that is 10 times smaller than that i.e. $0.26m^3/hr/m^2$. Ecological Building Systems have a graphic representation[3] showing that at this rate of leakage a new house has a leakage area equivalent to a hole-in-the-wall ATM cash machine, whereas a Passivhaus leakage area would be equivalent to a credit card.

This gives you a starting point. If you want more detail, I'm afraid it's well beyond my maths, so you'll need to research it.

HOW TO ACHIEVE AIRTIGHTNESS

In theory, achieving airtightness is pretty simple. It is just a matter of making sure there are no gaps where air can come through. 'Just', I hear myself say – such a loaded word!

In new extensions – if you are having a new extension built, then the architect should have included the airtightness line as part of the design, but it's worth making sure you understand where it sits. It won't be a straight line; just the connection between all the elements of the 'windproof jacket':

- how the walls join together
- no break between walls and the floor
- windows tightly fitted into the frame, continuing the airtight barrier
- pipes entering the house without leaving space for air to come with them.

One option is to wrap the extension in a vapour control membrane. If this is done at the outset, it is less of a headache than trying to join up lots of different materials to create the airtightness layer.

Even with a vapour control membrane, you'll need to take care where pipes bring services into the house from outside (service penetrations). It's tempting for plumbers and electricians to make holes that are significantly bigger than the pipes or cables going through them – which makes good sense for their ease of working, as long as they then do a thorough job of filling the gaps to stop air coming in.

The ideal way to overcome this problem is to have a service void designed into the wall and roof – a battened space behind the plasterboard – to carry the service pipes. Once the work is done, the void can be filled with insulation to prevent heat loss. Having the airtightness line sitting behind the service void (i.e. further into the wall) means you can alter the services without impacting the airtightness because you only have to breach the plasterboard.

When retrofitting – going back through an old house to address airtightness is another matter altogether. Not only were methods different at the time of building, but there is every chance that some slippage/subsidence will have taken place over the years. This means that there will be minuscule gaps at wall junctions, around doors, between wall and floor and around windows. As time goes by there may also be damage in pointing, leaving gaps where air can get in between the bricks.

If you're anything like us, you'll also have done other renovations over the years at a time when less attention was paid to the environment. It became glaringly obvious to us where air gaps from previous plumbing and lower levels of insulation contributed to our cold state.

It takes a bit of forensic investigation to work all this out. Get your perfectionist mindset on and go exploring. Sit in each room and consider every inch with a view to finding the gaps. Make the most of a windy day to feel for draughts – the extra pressure will show them up more easily. Notice every time your feet get cold and question where the cold air is coming in. You'll probably drive yourself up the wall for a while (or is that just me?) but it will pay off in the end.

Another option is to get an airtightness test done before you start the work. This will tell you where existing problem areas lie so they can be put right. It's also very satisfying to have a comparison when you get your final test done – gives you cause for celebration.

Once you have a list of actions, set about sorting each one or find a reliable and detailed handy person to help (and if you find a good one, let everyone know!). There are various ways to achieve this:

- additional insulation in large spaces − for us it was in the space under the sink kitchen cupboard − then making sure to seal up all the joins in the insulation batts
- expandable foam − environmentally this is a last resort, so do look into this fully before using it; it's pretty toxic stuff
- tapes designed to close up gaps − a perfect example for us was using Contega tape to seal between the walls and the floor before putting down the carpet.

And remember − if you manage a good level of airtightness, you must also sort out ventilation or you'll end up with condensation in your beautiful new place (see Chapter 10).

The three biggest risk areas for heat loss are:

- windows and doors
- holes through into the fabric of the house
- chimneys and fireplaces.

Windows

In a typical house, about one-third of the total heat loss in winter occurs through the windows. It will happen in two ways:

- air loss at the edges of the windows where they meet the frame − this is much more likely when the windows are old because of subsidence/shifting and/or wear of the seal between glass and frame

- warm air hitting the cold of the glass – this is the windows themselves, rather than airtightness, so see Chapter 12 for more about glazing.

Airtightness relies on the windows being really well fitted into the space. There must be a continuous airtight seal between the window and the house structure. This is best done at the outset but can also be added in later.

In new build extensions – installing the windows correctly is the job of the builder/window installer. Make sure they know your requirements with regard to airtightness. In a new build extension, with your builder on board, the precision should have been built in from the start. In this case, they'll know the importance of accurate fitting of windows and doors and they'll be able to support an external fitter on how the work needs to be done. The job should be pretty straightforward in a new build – with straight lines, new materials and modern knowledge.

In renovations – this is still the job of the builder or window installer, but this time there is the added frisson of an old building. Walls may not be straight, bricks will have odd bits broken off, the actual frame may be a different size at the top and bottom. The big difference is that nothing is a given. Decisions need to be made, on the hoof sometimes, about the best ways to go forward.

Given that many of the final decisions will come back to you as the owner, make sure you're informed about the elements that are most important to you – in this case, airtightness. If you can point to this as a requirement, then the builder/fitter will know what they need to do. If they are just going for something that fits the space and looks good, you are unlikely to get the precision you need.

Find out from your builder/fitter what their plans are. There are specific airtightness tapes that can be used – e.g. the Pro Clima[4] range, which is made for windows, doors and floor-wall connections. They are easy to use and more effective, durable and vapour permeable than expanding foam. They are also completely invisible once the window is installed.

Airtight doors

The same principles apply as for windows. The door itself can be the best on offer, but if it's not fitted properly into the space then you won't be airtight. Make sure you use an expert fitter who understands the principle and will focus on how the door fits into the space, using the appropriate tape to deliver airtightness.

If your doors are already fitted, then you can check for airtightness by:

- having an airtightness test that will tell you about the effectiveness of doors, windows and floorboards – the whole nine yards (see below)
- testing it yourself on a windy day – hold your hand to the join and see how much air is coming through. It will be most obvious on a windy day, but if you feel it then it will also be coming through on calm days, just more quietly
- borrowing a thermal imaging camera (see chapter 7) – this will tell you where cold spots are all around the house and show you where to start taking action.

There are a number of options for improving airtightness on an existing door:

- check that the door hinges fit tightly. If not, then this will skew the position of the door, allowing air to come in through variable gaps. Once the hinges are adjusted you will be able to take the next step

- research and find the best weather-proofing strip for your needs. Make sure it is fitted on all the doors that show up as having a draught. Include internal doors to cooler areas – the door to the utility room, the hall, downstairs loo…

- attach a door sweep – a strip of brush material that is fitted along the bottom of a door to seal the gap between the door and the floor. If it sticks against the floor, then you need to trim it, but do this a bit at a time or you might end up back where you started

- get a letterbox draught excluder if you don't have one already. And remember to apologise to the post person for their nipped fingers!

- consider whether you really need a cat flap. It might be hard to imagine life without one, but maybe you could have one cat flap into a cold space, such as a porch, utility room or garage, and then another from there into the main house. If you're really serious about airtightness (or just want your mind blown a bit) you can look up Passivhaus cat flaps[5]. These are installed in the wall and have a sort of air lock system with a flap at either side of the wall – but be warned, the price tag is very high.

––––––

Trust the experts?

It was a great day when our new triple-glazed windows arrived. I'd been so looking forward to this – weatherproof at last! But then the installer asked us where we wanted the windows to sit in the frame. There were so many moments like this on the building site that was home: a question comes from one person, soon to be followed by three others and everyone wants the answer immediately otherwise work will be held up for ages. We'd assumed the window installer would be an expert so the question took us totally by surprise. We'd been without windows for so long – gaping holes covered by old doors, batts of insulation and used plastic sheeting – so any stumbling block now felt like the end of the world.

From what I know now, we'd needed to put the question back to him as the expert. Instead we let ourselves get bumped into a decision and suggested following the pattern of the established windows. Of course, the architect visited the next day and told us they were in the wrong place.

There was a large gap between the window and the end of the wall – never mind air leakage, this was a tsunami. The risk to airtightness of such a mistake was enormous. Of course, we were able to fill this with expanded foam insulation material (yuk), but our job could have been so much easier. And I'm left with that doubt – are they actually working properly or not?

So my advice to you: be prepared. Work out what your questions need to be and lead with those. And if an expert expects you to make the decision – pause, breathe and ask for their informed opinion. And if the worst happens and there is a delay, remember, this will all be forgotten as soon as the relevant work is completed. House renovation is just like childbirth – you forget the pain once the finished article is in situ. Until the next time, of course!

Holes through the fabric of the house

Wherever services come into the house there is a risk of air leakage. The list of possible leakage points is long so it's worth researching[6] online. I guarantee there will be some places you've never thought of. One that took me by surprise was the ceiling roses where electric cables come in for the lights. Then there are all the pipes that come into sinks, bath, shower etc, holes for the sash window rope, boiler flues... the list goes on.

Make sure your builder is on-side with this one. You are asking for very close attention to detail in a way that may not yet come naturally. Traditionally, the emphasis will be on the task at hand – plumbing in the sink, fitting your new lights, inserting a waste pipe into the sub-floor void; they'll just want to get the job done, so checking back on airtightness may not come high on the list. If you've had the conversation ahead of time and/or you check on work as it goes along, the task will be easier. Take it from me, filling gaps around the water pipes once the kitchen is in place is a much bigger job than doing it at the time.

Important: every house has major holes in the fabric that must never be blocked up – the air bricks. So be zealous everywhere else but leave these free. They are doing a vital job of ventilating below the floor and dispelling gases such as radon and it is possible to expel draughts without disrupting this airflow. Just treat the sub-floor void at air brick level as 'outside' and apply tape so draughts don't leak through.

Chimneys and fireplaces

I hate this one. An open fire is such a treat – comforting on a Sunday afternoon after a long, wet walk, toasting crumpets with the kids, sending letters up the chimney to Father Christmas. Eco renovation means rethinking all that.

A chimney is a dirty great hole linking the outside to the inside of your house, so of course it's going to bring in masses of cold air. Any time the fire isn't lit, cold air will come down the chimney. When the fire is lit it will suck in warm air and send it up the chimney together with a lot of the heat, while also pulling up other draughts that might be lurking in the room. And if the chimney can't do all of that, your fire won't draw and you're lost anyway.

There are different ways to address the problem of the wind tunnel that is your chimney:

- Take the whole thing out. If you don't use the fire, this has to be the best option. Anything else is trying to make it less bad. But it's a dirty business and you may not be up for that level of change.
- You can fit a fireplace damper that sits above the firebox and can close fully and create a tight seal. I know we had one of those from the times I tried to light a fire without opening it – there was SMOKE in the room!
- A chimney draft excluder will fill the space within your chimney, so stops the cold air coming down into your room. There are a number of options, so search the internet and see what might fit your requirements. Some are made of plastic and less durable, so take care to buy the one that is environmentally friendly. Not much point in managing airtightness while creating plastic waste doing it. The good thing about these is they can easily be removed when you want to use the fire. They have a handle a bit like an umbrella that is easy to use. Ones made from felted wool are good at preventing heat loss while still allowing a small amount of ventilation.

- Install a fire box. Quality doors create a strong seal that improves the efficiency of the fire, as well as stopping draughts when the fire is out. Just make sure it fits very snuggly into the space with no air leakage around it.
- Install a wood-burning stove. You'll create a lot of warmth and can watch the logs burn, but crucially the chimney is sealed up around the stove flue. Wood-burning stoves have been subject to debate over whether they do more harm than good, based on the soot particles they produce, which contribute to air pollution. However, if you plan to have regular fires that produce soot anyway, then a stove is a better alternative. They are more efficient, so you'll burn fewer logs, and if you can source dry well-seasoned logs locally then this is a better solution than burning fossil fuels to heat your home.
- And if you have your heart set on using an open fire, then make sure you have a chimney cowl. Not only do they improve draw from the fire, but they reduce down draughts. This is not a life-changing solution, but it will make some improvement to those freezing draughts from the unlit fire when the wind blows.

Sit down near the fire and think it through. If you're already going to be doing some work on your house, could this be added to the list? Would you miss the fire very much if it wasn't there? If the answer is a heartfelt 'yes', consider the options for reducing draughts. If you're really serious about airtightness, then removing the chimney has to come high on the list of options.

Chim chiminey...

Our old house has two chimneys – a fire was the only source of heat in the late 1800s and early 1900s. We were always very conscious of the cold draughts they created, but just accepted it as normal for an old house. One morning during the renovation, I woke up to John suggesting we take the chimney breast out of the dining room – which, of course, also meant in the room above. It took me and the builder by surprise – but we were both getting used to this by now. The work started a couple of days later.

Sometimes I'm really slow on the uptake. Why didn't it occur to me that removing a chimney that's been in place since 1901 was going to be a dirty and smelly business? Tucked away in the front room, alongside loads of furniture and 'stuff', I worked away on my 'to-do' list, until I needed the loo. The only way out was through the offending room. I'd like to tell you what my eyes beheld, but I couldn't see a thing. The dust was so thick and the smell of accumulated coal, wood and damp was revolting.

We moved in with our daughter for the rest of the week after that – and stayed for one month. There are just some things that are too much to live through, even for us.

But it was a good choice. One major draught out of the way for good. We still struggle with the other chimney – so hard to give up the fire. Even with a high-precision fire box, draughts come through. Just as with windows, there is the fire box itself plus the space the fire box fits into. It's the latter we still have to sort out, so watch this space.

AIRTIGHTNESS TESTING

If you're serious about airtightness this is absolutely the way to go. It's the best way to confirm how well the airtightness line is working. A large fan is positioned in a door frame and sealed into place, then all the acceptable openings are sealed up – e.g. ventilation fans, doors, windows etc. Once the house is fully sealed, the fan is switched on, drawing air into the house through any remaining openings.

When to have an airtightness test

Ideally, it's best to think in terms of more than one airtightness test. For a Passivhaus[7] there will be three tests – when the building shell is complete, at the second fix (this is when the services have been installed, but not yet covered up) and a final test once the building is complete and ready to be occupied.

It's not a requirement for a renovation or retrofit – only new houses are legally required to run an airtightness test. But for those of us who are serious about making our homes environmentally friendly, it's the perfect way to identify the areas that need specific work and to check up on what we've done so far. Certainly, we found it to be invaluable. It's not so expensive in the scheme of things and it highlights all the areas that will irritate you if left unattended. But please do organise it when you can still reach the areas of greatest risk and before you set about decorating and making the place look good – take it from one who knows. Arghhh!

What is a good airtightness score?

Most new builds these days will score a $5m^2/hrm^2@50Pa$ and a really well-built new house could come in as low as $3m^2/hrm^2@50Pa$ – although the latter will require quality ventilation if condensation and mould are to be avoided.

Clearly the lower the score, the better for the environment.

Before your airtightness test take time to check the following:

- All fixtures and fittings, including lights and sockets, are installed and well sealed.
- Every service penetration is sealed.
- All plumbing work is complete, with water in the traps.
- The join between walls and floors is sealed with tape, and the skirting board put back. Belt and braces would then be to seal up the join between the floor and the base of the skirting board.
- Bathrooms and kitchens are fully fitted and mastic sealed.
- All external and internal windows and doors are installed and closable.
- The loft hatch is fitted and sealed.

Our first airtightness test

Our architect mentioned the need for airtightness in the extension, but sadly we didn't pay enough attention at the time. Once we understood more fully, we wanted to run the test, but with so much work going on in the house it was easy to keep waiting for the best time. Now we know that the best time is before you start doing all the pretty stuff, so you can still make changes to the basic fabric of the house.

Finally, when we heard that the front room carpet had arrived and a day was planned to lay it down, I realised this was it – we had to get the test done while we had the chance to make adjustments under the floor, if needed.

I called Jostec[8], a national company, that stepped up to the plate and put us in the diary for a few days later and John spent a day blocking up all the little holes we knew about. At this point we were feeling hopeful and just a tiny bit smug. Especially when the tester, Jim, said how rare it is for anyone to want a test just so they can improve things. He'd expected we were being told to do this for a loan of some sort. But oh dear, pride really does come before a fall!

The process requires a huge fan to be put into a doorway so that air can be sucked out of the house, causing more air to be sucked in through any holes or gaps. Having read quite a bit about it, I imagined us having to stand in the garden while it was done – I assumed we wouldn't be able to breathe inside. I also expected the computer to show all the places where air was coming in.

Once Jim set up the machine, with a little difficulty in our double doors, the process began. Of course, it didn't rid the house of oxygen – I was being far too dramatic – instead we were able to go around the house with him feeling for draughts. It was a bit alarming – because of the strength of the suction, any draught we found felt dreadful, whereas under normal circumstances we would hardly have noticed it.

I'm so pleased we did it – it was such an eye opener. We did need to seal up between the front room floorboards. In fact we put down an additional airtight membrane over the floor to make sure we'd caught them all. We found draughts all over the place that we didn't know about. Even where the original sash windows had been refurbished, there was air coming up through the rope hole. Not to mention through the pipe holes for the ASHP.

Then we got the reading – 9.5m³/hrm²@50Pa. So disappointed. Jim assured us that in a house as old as this we were never going to get a really good reading. But given how much work we'd done, we had really hoped for better than that. So the work continues. At least now we know where the gaps are and we are slowly making our way through them. And when we have done as much as we know about, we'll get Jim back and try again.

SUMMARY

- Airtightness is an important part of creating an eco house.
- Insulation without airtightness will still be very draughty and therefore cold.
- Airtightness is about draughts, joins, holes around pipes and light sockets – all the little gaps that are so easily created in a renovation project.
- You need to get your builder on board from the outset – this is nitpicky work and unless they know how serious you are, they may be tempted to cut corners.
- You can get a test that shows clearly where your draughts are. It will give you a rating of how effective your airtightness is.
- Don't wait until the end of your renovation to have a test done – you may have work to do and you don't want to mess up your lovely new décor.

1. http://www.environmentaldesignpocketbook.com
2. http://www.passivhaustrust.org.uk/UserFiles/File/Technical%20Papers/Good%20Practice%20Guide%20to%20Airtightness%20v10.6-compressed(1).pdf
3. http://www.ecologicalbuildingsystems.com/post/what-airtightness
4. https://proclima.com/products
5. http://www.greenbuildingadvisor.com/article/a-passive-house-door-for-pets
6. http://www.greenspec.co.uk/building-design/refurb-airtightness
7. https://www.passivhaustrust.org.uk
8. https://jostec.co.uk/services/air-tightness-testing/

CHAPTER 9
BREATHABILITY

The first thing to understand is that although we call it breathability, we're actually talking about the passive transfer of moisture. I know – doesn't make much sense to me either, but there you go.

If you can recall any of the science you learned at school, you'll know that air holds moisture and the amount of water held will depend on the temperature of the air plus the moisture available for it to pick up. So the more people you have in the house and the more activity there is, the more moisture there will be.

When warm air created in the house hits a cold surface – glass, cold wall, tiled floor – it can no longer hold the same amount of water, so the moisture condenses onto the cold surface as water droplets. If this goes on for long enough, the dampness created starts to grow the black mould we all recognise from corners of shower cubicles and cold windows.

Here's an interesting statistic – the average family can produce up to 15 litres of water vapour in one day just through their normal activities: washing, bathing, cooking, drying clothes, sweating, breathing… That's a lot of water and it has to go somewhere.

Important: it's not possible to address breathability on its own, you have to address it in conjunction with **airtightness, insulation and ventilation**. All these elements are directly linked, so read those chapters alongside this one. Understanding the inter-relationship from the outset will help you to ask the pertinent questions at the right time.

UNDERSTANDING MOISTURE

There are two main sources of moisture in a home:

- external sources
- internal condensation.

External sources

This is caused when water from outside makes its way inside. Building failure is the most likely cause – when something has become worn and no longer fit for purpose or if mistakes have been made at the outset. For instance, rainwater seeping in through a broken roof tile, driving wind forcing wet air through a crack in the brickwork, rising damp, leaking surfaces or appliances, a break in external render or something as simple as blocked guttering.

Building problems are generally fairly easy to assess and repair. It may not be cheap but it's possible to see what's happening and take steps to put it right.

———

Let's get a ladder

I remember sitting by the fire with my two young daughters watching **Neighbours** *at the end of a school* *day – as we did in those days. It was really miserable and rainy outside, which added to the comfy feel of the room – until water started pouring in from above the bay window.*

John was away working and I had absolutely no idea what was causing the stream of water. Fortunately, my youngest daughter – who was about 10 at the time – enjoyed spending time with Dad doing jobs. So she immediately thought of the guttering. "Come on," she said, "let's get a ladder."

I felt such a wimp, but also a proud mum, as she climbed up the ladder and stuck her hands into the gutter, pulling out all the dead leaves and mould. She had been completely right and her efforts sent the water back to the path it should have been following all along.

This wasn't a building failure – it was our mainte-nance failure that saw the stormy night flowing into the house. And we never did see the end of **Neighbours***!*

Internal condensation

This is a different matter altogether. Modern houses are full of moisture because they're generally very warm so the air can hold more vapour.[1] Central heating means that the air can hang onto:

- moisture from the air we breathe out
- the steam we create through cooking
- moisture from showers and baths
- water released by house plants

- the spills and sweat of daily life…

All that work to make the house airtight removes any easy exits for the wet air, so now we have to deal with the moisture before it does damage to the fabric of the house.

New builds deal with moisture by using waterproof, non-breathable materials – dense bricks, cement mortars and renders, waterproof masonry paints and damp-proof courses. When done correctly, they keep the water out. But as many new home owners will tell you, they don't deal well with internal condensation. Witness the number of dehumidifiers available online.

Old houses are constructed very differently. Anything pre-war will be built of stone, brick or timber; with earth- or lime-based mortars; and often covered with earth- or lime-based plaster, render or paint. These materials allow moisture to penetrate the building fabric from both sides and then evaporate away. They are 'breathable'.

This breathability means an old building doesn't need to be waterproof or completely dry. The combination of breathable materials and the built-in lack of airtightness keeps the air moving, so paradoxically the house feels dry, even if it is sometimes draughty. Externally, porous materials dry in the wind and sun. Internally, air moves out of the house through the roof, windows and chimneys as the pressure gradient created by the temperature difference between the warm air inside and the cool air outside drives moisture through the walls.

So when it comes to renovating an old house, especially when we want to be more eco in the process, we have to keep moisture in mind because everything we set out to do is going to disrupt the natural flow of the original house.

For a very clear description of breathability, try this blog[2].

BREATHABILITY IS ABOUT WET AIR

Using breathable materials – such as lime mortars or plasters – means the building is better able to deal with moisture, passively allowing damp air to pass through the wall and releasing it into the atmosphere, reducing the risk of damage.

The closest I've come to a simple explanation is another clothes metaphor: you know those smart workout shirts that 'wick' away the sweat? Throughout the workout, sweat is carried through the shirt into the air, where it becomes vapour and you have a fighting chance of not being the BO monster when you get home. No wicking and all the sweat is trapped wet against your skin, leaving the pong for all to experience.

In a building, the breathable materials are the snazzy clothes that can wick away the vapour – breath, steam, sweat – from inside the house and allow it to pass through into the garden in its dry form.

Vapour and its ability to condense is the bane of every building and sadly it's often the new builds that are most affected. Insulation and airtightness are sometimes addressed well, but breathability and ventilation are either forgotten or inadequate, leaving a trail of black mould in their wake.

What does this mean for your building work?

You need to decide at the outset either to build with modern, rigid, non-breathable materials that block the movement of moisture altogether or to go with breathable materials.

It sounds like a no-brainer to go with the waterproof/non-breathable materials of new builds – why bother `with anything else if this style of building can keep the house safe from the elements? Sadly that's too simplistic. It misses the fact that when people are in the house, they'll produce moisture just by virtue of being alive and it all has to be dealt with.

Breathable materials will do this naturally, allowing the air to move between elements carrying vapour with it. So although it is difficult to understand, breathable materials will be better for both the building and the people in the long run.

If you do decide to go with non-breathable, then it is even more important to have a really good ventilation system. That is the only way to overcome the problem of excess moisture with nowhere to go. So please do read chapter 10, which will give you a start and the questions to ask to help you overcome the risk of the non-breathable.

Go the whole hog

If you decide to go with breathable materials, then you need to go all the way. The two styles won't work together – any attempt to mix them can leave moisture stuck somewhere in the system with no way out. If there is a mix for some reason, you may end up with damp and moisture within the insulation, which will cause it to bunch up and reduce its effectiveness.

The problems won't arise quickly but by the time you see the effects – peeling paint, bubbling wallpaper, wall feeling cold to the touch, damp smell, stains and mould – it's too late. Then you just have to strip it all back and start again.

Getting your head around breathability will enable you to ask the relevant questions of your architect or project manager, including:

- If extending, is the wall going to be breathable and will it match the other parts of the building? Lime-based mortar is what you're looking for – this is the part that's breathable. Cement mortar is non-breathable.

- Are they familiar with breathable plaster and plasterboard?
- What about the external render – if you are changing this as part of the renovation, then you need to make sure it is a breathable render. What will be the impact of a combination of a new interior with the existing exterior render?
- Ask them to talk you through the wall from inside to outside, explaining the breathability of each layer, so you can be sure that it all fits together.

————

Damn it!

We were doing so well and thought we finally had it cracked. We'd used all breathable materials – the original brick and plaster, wood and Pavaflex insulation, lime plaster and breathable paint. It was all going really well and we were close to having the house to ourselves again. I couldn't quite imagine it, if I'm honest.

It was the final stage – painting outside so that the new extension would finally look like it belonged. As so often happened, the decorator asked what paint we wanted just as I was about to walk out of the door to pick up my grandson from nursery. So instead of stopping to think, I agreed we'd go with the robust external paint he was used to using. It looks great and we were happy with the result.

Honestly, I only realised our mistake when I started writing this book. Suddenly the reality pinged in my brain. We had blown all that careful work by putting a layer of non-breathable paint on the outside of the house. I can't believe it!

It's not irredeemable, thank heavens. At least there are only two of us living and breathing in the space and the changes won't be instant, but this sits right at the top of the 'to-do' list. We have to bite the bullet and remove the paint, starting all over again. Oh joy – scaffolding, mess, noise – the price of rushing a decision.

———

SUMMARY

- Breathability is actually about moisture.
- Insulation and airtightness need breathability and ventilation to balance them. If you ignore the presence of moisture you store up trouble for the future.
- Breathable materials create a passive means for moisture to be absorbed and released by the building fabric.
- Don't mix the two together or you'll store up problems. Once you start going breathable you need to stay breathable and the same with non-breathable.

---

1. http://www.ecomerchant.co.uk/news/breathable-building-airtightness-explained#_ftnref1
2. http://www.greenspec.co.uk/building-design/importance-of-breathability-in-old-buildings

CHAPTER 10
VENTILATION

I f you're retrofitting an old house, you'll never have had to think about ventilation. We've talked about this before – old houses manage moisture by being really leaky. They may not be warm, but they are certainly well supplied with fresh air. All of which is cause for a good moan but, on the whole, it's just par for the course.

You probably have draught excluders, you'll check the windows are closed tight, wear warm slippers, add an extra jumper. But as soon as you go for a retrofit, all this changes. Now it's a matter of pride that air gaps are filled up, the airtightness line is firmly in place, all cold bridges are covered with insulation and the building is breathable. Great stuff – but now you don't have air flow and you still need it to manage the levels of water vapour. Arghhh!

Important: it's not possible to address ventilation on its own – you have to address it in conjunction with **breathability, insulation and airtightness**. All these elements are directly linked, so read those chapters alongside this one. Understanding the inter-relationship from the outset will help you to ask the pertinent questions at the right time.

Your house will deal with moisture in two ways:

1. Some moisture is absorbed and released by the breathable materials in the walls, roof and floor (see Chapter 9).
2. Most of the moisture expelled from the house is driven out through ventilation, where water droplets suspended in the air are carried away as the air moves outside.

It's this movement of air that we're talking about here and the issue is all about control. A leaky house manages moisture well, but you have little or no control of the air that comes in – you are dependent on conditions outside. A windy day will leave you shivering from the draughts and on a hot still day, you'll feel stifled and uncomfortable. You have no way of determining where the air goes. It will continue on its merry way from warm to cold regardless. It can just as easily move from the kitchen or bathroom – moisture-creating spaces – to the bedroom, creating condensation and possibly mould.

So what we're looking for is ventilation you can control. When formulated properly it will give you so much more than a load of fresh air floating through your house.

WHY DO WE NEED AIR CIRCULATION?

Look up anything on ventilation and you'll find wise words explaining that we need air circulation, but no one says why. So here's my understanding:

Imagine your house as a closed box full of air. The air will circulate within the box but have no way of escaping to the outside or allowing fresh air to come in and take its place. In this scenario there are five issues:

1. lack of oxygen
2. condensation
3. smells
4. volatile organic compounds (VOCs)
5. allergens.

Lack of oxygen

This is pretty self-explanatory: oxygen keeps us alive and there are a number of ways that a lack of fresh air impacts us day to day:

- coughing and difficulty breathing
- sneezing or allergic reactions
- skin dryness or irritation
- headaches or nausea
- dust build-up
- hot and cold spots
- unpleasant odour
- drowsiness and lack of concentration.

It's quite a list and they're all issues that we want to avoid. The problem is that it's easy to forget ventilation. Because we can't see air, it's easy to forget how important it is.

I suspect most people will recognise the impact more from being in public buildings where windows don't open. I always experience that first breath of fresh air after long business meetings in airtight rooms as being cool and sweet smelling, like freesias. It feels so wonderful and makes me realise I don't appreciate it enough. Then I'm comfortable again and then the lack of oxygen goes to the back of my mind.

Condensation

I have first-hand experience of the horrors of condensation. My first adult home had metal-framed, single-glazed windows, so I have very clear memories of waking up in the morning with water streaming down the glass. And worse still, in winter we regularly had frost on the inside. Of course, I'm talking early 1970s, so for most of us those days are long gone. But still we have to take care to avoid the risk of water inside the house.

———

The dreaded curtain mould

I saw a perfect example of this recently when visiting a friend. She had recently moved to a lovely new build flat – warm and cosy with the added benefit of a joint ventilation system to keep the air fresh. It had huge windows and faced south so it could get really warm in summer, which led to an increased risk of water vapour as the day cooled.

But it soon became clear that she had a problem. When the full-length curtains in the bedroom were held out from the wall, there were clear patches of black mould. The situation was made worse because she preferred to sleep with the window closed at night, when her breath was producing a constant flow of water vapour. And with nowhere to go and nothing to do, the vapour focused on making mould.

This can be a problem when a ventilation system serves numerous flats and can't be adapted to the personal needs of each resident. Opening the window is an obvious quick win but that doesn't suit every-one. Moving the curtains regularly is also a way round. But without an effective ventilation system it is always going to be a challenge to keep the space condensation- and mould-free.

And just to reassure you – I don't go sneaking into bedrooms looking behind the curtains – I was invited. So if I ever visit you, you're quite safe – I promise to stay well away from your mould!

The joy of a fresh-smelling house

We create smells in the house just by being – it's impossible not to. Ever had that experience where someone walks into a room and tells you it smells just like your home? And you probably didn't even know your place had a smell. When I was a kid, the smell was of coal dust, Wright's Coal Tar soap and cooked cabbage. In the first years of marriage it was rugby kit, burned food and Napisan sanitiser. More recently damp dog, garlic and freshly baked bread.

The natural smells of life are not just an indicator of how you spend your time. They also show that the air needs changing. We know enough to put an extractor fan in the kitchen, bathroom and loo, but that's about all that is automatic thinking.

Then there are VOCs

Volatile organic compounds – this was a new one on me. I can't say I'd heard of them until I began taking a more thorough look into ventilation. We're talking about the invisible gases that build up from cosmetics, air fresheners, hairspray, cleaning fluids and the chemicals released from plastics in your home – window casing, PIR insulation, paint etc (known as off-gassing). Research[1] from the Environmental Protection Agency show the air inside homes could be significantly more polluted than it is outdoors.

We can deal with this by changing the cleaning and hygiene products we use in the home – go eco and you'll immediately reduce your home pollution. But you also need to install some form of ventilation – at least once your home becomes better sealed.

Managing allergens

Damp and mould can be triggers for asthma. So can dust mites, which thrive in high humidity. Then there is pollen in the spring and summer, which causes so much distress through hayfever. Keep changing the air and you reduce the allergens in your home.

WHAT NEEDS TO HAPPEN?

However efficient your retrofit, it's highly unlikely you'll create an entirely airtight box. There are too many variables in old houses for this to be possible. But you will certainly have a much tighter box and a greatly reduced inflow of fresh air. So you do have to find a way to exchange air regularly and reduce the risk of condensation. There are a number of options:

Uncontrolled ventilation – we've talked a lot about this: air that looks after itself and just pops up wherever it can manage to get in. From under the floor, through the letterbox or cat flap, draughty doorways – you know what I'm talking about. It's worked fine for years, but now you know it's costing you a fortune and leaving you pretty cold into the bargain.

Partially controlled ventilation – this is a controlled version of the old house. Instead of natural air vents, inbuilt openings are used to get air in when needed.

- **Open a window** – most obvious and easy to do is to open the window. It works really well, especially in summer when the weather is warm – and it will change the air in the room quickly. However, a lot of heat is lost through the opening and it takes energy to build back up to a comfortable level, by which time you probably need to open the window again.

- **Tilt and turn windows** – windows that open fully in the normal way but can also be opened a small amount to allow for air change while losing less heat. All the same concerns apply as for a standard opening window; it just takes a little longer to get really cold. In spring–summer it works well by allowing in a small amount of fresh air, but it is certainly not the best for an eco home.
- **Trickle vents** – this is a small grid with an opening slider, set at the top of double- and triple-glazed windows. These are kept open constantly to allow air to trickle into your house at a reasonable rate so you don't feel a cold draught, giving you a balanced environment. However, it still means you are losing the heat you have so carefully created. Also, it is a small amount of air, so it may still be necessary to open a window as well.

All these options are operated manually, so rely on occupants to open and close them to minimise heat loss.

Controlled ventilation – there are different ways to control ventilation:

- **Extractor fans** work by forcing air out of a space to remove unwanted odours, particulates, smoke, moisture and other contaminants that may be present in the air. This is the sort of fan we put in bathrooms, toilets and kitchens. They work well to freshen up the air but they also steal a great deal of warmth and bring cold draughts into the room.
- **Single-room heat recovery ventilation fans** move air into and out of rooms consistently. The fans

are left on 24/7 and have variable speeds that change according to the humidity in the room. The heat recovery option means that up to 95% of the heat in your room is passed from the outgoing warm air pipe to the incoming cold air pipe so it can bring warm fresh air into the room. You can have as many of these heat recovery fans as you need and they come in different sizes to suit the square footage of your room. If you're good with tech, they can also be linked up and managed from an app on your smart phone.

- **A mechanical ventilation heat recovery system (MVHR)** is a whole home ventilation system that extracts stale air and brings in fresh filtered air. It also retains up to 95% of the warmth from the house during the exchange of air. It is a very efficient system but does require space for a main unit to sit (usually in the loft) and chunky ducts that carry the clean air around the house. It must be designed by a specialist to make sure the runs are as short and as efficient as possible once it is served by smart technology. It's ideal when building a new house from scratch, when it can be included in the design. However, it is rarely relevant to an old-house retrofit because of the difficulty of hiding the ducting in the fabric of the building and the fact that the building needs to be extremely airtight and well insulated for it to work.

- **Demand controlled ventilation (DCV)** or humidity sensitive MEV (mechanical extract ventilation) responds to the internal environment using sensors to check humidity and carbon dioxide levels, so the fans only run when they are needed. It's very efficient in terms of energy, but doesn't include heat recovery like MVHR and single room units, so it's not as popular in the UK as in other more temperate countries.

———

Look what I found!

It was one of those fortuitous internet searches. We knew we needed ventilation and we knew about MVHR. It sounded fantastic, but there was no way it would fit into our old house. So I had to get on the case and find something that would work. Eventually I came across a single-room heat recovery extractor fan. It was SO exciting! (Well I did say I was a building bore.)

They really did seem to be just what we needed. Now we just had to decide which one and how many. They didn't cost the earth, but neither were they cheap off the shelf at B&Q, so John was thinking about cutting down the number. Me – I wanted them everywhere to be on the safe side. And it wasn't easy to find an expert who could adjudicate.

We ended up with two downstairs: a large one in the open-plan kitchen / dining room / family area and a small one in the sitting room; and three upstairs – so far – bathroom, study and spare room. Since we close the door and open the window at night in our bedroom we decided we didn't need one there, although we are watching very carefully to see if that decision is correct.

Two unexpected learnings: number one – they are brilliant for getting the clothes dry. Without radiators to put the washing on, I had no idea how we'd manage in the winter. And don't tell me to use a tumble dryer. All that energy? You must be joking! But I needn't have worried – a clothes horse in the spare bedroom works like magic.

Learning number two belongs to my grandson. He hates the sound of the smoke alarm, so as soon as I start to fry anything he shouts for the fan to be put on boost. "Don't set the noise off, Granny, put on the fan!" He knows frying's not my thing, and he knows how well the fan works. Good lad!

———

Given this is a book about retrofitting, your most likely option will be the single-room heat recovery ventilation units, so a few thoughts about what to look for before you choose:

- Noise levels – they run 24/7 and they'll be in your main living areas, so find out how loud they are.
- Decide whether you need them to link together – some will do this if you're up for understanding how to work the app.
- Can you change the sensor level? They have a humidity sensor and you may or may not be able to change this to suit your needs. This is important and ensures you get more powerful ventilation only when you need it.
- Design – how do they look and what will fit into your décor?
- Position – clearly they need to be placed on an outside wall, so make sure you have somewhere that is unobtrusive and effective.

There are a number of different options on the market. We began by looking at Envirovent[2], which is British-made so less air miles. With a single-room machine you can put one in and follow up with more if it works for you. This is what we decided to do. At this stage we were going for just two – in the kitchen and the bathroom. We were clearly still thinking standard ventilation and not yet really taking in the needs of an airtight-ish house.

As time went on and we understood more clearly, we discovered the Blauberg[3] technical experts, who were very helpful and gave us advice on what we needed and where.

The Blauberg allows us to adjust the humidity sensor. This is particularly relevant in the bathroom. Use the shower or bath, or even flush the loo, and the Envirovent was going like the clappers. It was more efficient than we needed in those areas.

So now we have a Blauberg in the bathroom, with the humidity sensor turned down to a more useable level and adjusted to boost when humidity is high; in the kitchen, so we can use the boost when cooking requires; and in the sitting room. The Envirovents are in the spare room, drying the washing overnight, and in the study.

Do I still need a cooker hood?

I am often asked if we still needed a cooker hood in the kitchen as well as the ventilation fan. The answer is yes. The hob extractor fan removes the smells of cooking as well as the extreme moisture produced from boiling and simmering and it does so at source, making for swift removal of the water vapour. Depending where your hob is in relation to the vent this would be a much longer job without a hob extractor, because the vent would take time to mop up the sudden increase in water vapour in the room.

The ventilation units described here are just our choice and there are of course other options out there. Vent-Axia[4] make them, as do Siegenia[5] and I'm sure there are others.

SUMMARY

- A leaky house has its own passive ventilation system with natural draughts.
- Once the house is airtight, ventilation needs to be included in a controlled way.
- We can control ventilation by opening windows but that costs in heat loss.
- Heat recovery ventilation extracts the heat from the outgoing air and passes it to the colder incoming air, saving the heat while removing the moisture.
- You will still need an extractor fan for your hob as well as the vent to remove smells and steam more quickly.

---

1. https://www.parliament.uk/globalassets/documents/post/postpn366_indoor_air_quality.pdf
2.
3. http://www.blauberg.co.uk/en/blauberg-uk-domestic-ventilation-product-range/single-room-heat-recovery-units
4. http://www.vent-axia.com/range/mechanical-ventilation-with-heat-recovery-mvhr
5. http://www.siegenia.com/gb/landingpages/srhr

CHAPTER 11
HEATING AND SOLAR ENERGY

N ow we get to the point of the whole exercise – creating a house that is warm and comfortable to live in without costing the earth.

The first big decision is what sort of heating to go for and a useful measure to understand is the coefficient of performance (COP). This is expressed in a ratio: how much heat is given out in relation to the energy required to produce it. So just as you want more miles per gallon from a car, you want a high coefficient of performance from your heating system, meaning you get more units of heat produced for every unit of energy used.

There are two main sources of fuel to consider in the domestic setting:

- gas – typically a boiler and central heating system
- electricity – storage heaters, heat pumps and photovoltaic (PV/solar).

GAS HEATING

This is a heating system we're all familiar with so there's not much to say. It works well, has been reasonably low in cost (although this is changing fast) and condensing boilers make it more environmentally friendly. Because gas heats water quickly to a high temperature, radiators can be small, unobtrusive and nowadays quite funky.

If you live off the natural gas network you probably use liquid petroleum gas (LPG) with boilers/condensing boilers, which is highly efficient. It has to be delivered by road, which can cause problems with supply, however, and the storage tanks are large and unattractive, so you need plenty of space around the house to hide them away.

Gas is becoming increasingly expensive for households and the earth. As a fossil fuel, it must be removed from the ground, which brings untold damage. Plus, when it is burned, it releases all the carbon the coal has held so effectively over millions of years, adding to our already calamitous carbon load. As such, it is the biggest source of carbon emissions from the home.

Gas also has a low COP. For every unit of fuel used by a condensing boiler – the most efficient gas boiler – only 1.08 units of heat are produced. So pretty much one for one.

Because of the climate crisis, gas boilers overall (including LPG) will be phased out in new homes by 2025. To my knowledge, there is no date set yet for replacing existing gas boilers, but the statistics are clear that gas must go. Gas causes up to 30% of our greenhouse emissions, so anyone with any concern about the environment is going to want to change as soon as they can.

Efficient gas boilers also make us lazy about insulation – because they heat the home so quickly and effectively, it's easy to believe that insulation is a nice-to-have rather than a must-have, even to the point of new homes failing to reach the required environmental expectations. Not to mention that home gas boilers collectively produce eight times as much nitrogen dioxide as all our power plants put together, an air pollutant linked to tens of thousands of early deaths a year in the UK.

ELECTRIC HEATING

Just the thought of storage heaters sparks memories from my first real home in the early 1970s. Huge tin boxes filled with heavy bricks to hold the heat. They came on at night when electricity was cheap and warmed the house until about 4pm, when it gradually cooled down and we spent an evening with the gas fire on to ward off the cold.

Of course, these days heaters are significantly more efficient. They have thermostats, 24/7 programmable timers plus temperature controls and fans to help distribute the heat. New high-end storage heaters retain more heat than traditional models – up to 45% 24 hours after they were last charged, which seems to deal with the cold evenings issue. Although the storage heaters work on Economy 7 and 10 (cheaper night-time electricity), you can also fit electric radiators that work with standard electricity tariffs, so you can switch them on and off whenever you want.

If you are served by a renewable energy provider there will be some benefit environmentally, in which case you can lower your carbon footprint.

However, around 40% of electricity in the UK is generated in gas-fired power stations, so any increase in the price of gas will also be reflected in the cost of electricity. This should make Economy 7 or Economy 10 a solid option, but sadly the tariffs overall are higher than on standard single-rate electricity. You do get cheaper heating at night but running appliances during the day can be expensive. And you can't just switch on the system to warm the house up if the weather suddenly turns cold. You will always have to wait for the following night for any additional heat in the house.

With regard to monetary cost, electricity prices have traditionally been approximately three to four times higher than gas per unit of energy, so previously it wasn't a good choice from a price perspective. Now this is changing, with gas quickly catching up and both gas and electricity prices likely to stay high. In terms of the COP, both have a ratio of 1:1 – giving you just one unit of heat for every unit of fuel you put in, which means you're paying a high price for the heat you need.

RENEWABLE ENERGY SOURCES

Using renewable energy from air, sun, wind or water is clearly the best way forward for the environment and when installed in a well-insulated and airtight house can also be much better for your purse. The most common options are the air source heat pump (ASHP) and the ground source heat pump (GSHP)

Air source heat pumps

This was the spur for all the work we did. It's taken me a while to understand how the machine works and I did have concerns given the conversations I'd seen on Facebook, but I can truthfully say that, now it's in place, we are both really pleased.

The beauty of the ASHP is that it draws heat from the air, providing more heat energy than the electrical energy used to operate it. It works like a fridge in reverse, using the same process of heat exchange. The fridge discards the heat (the coils at the back of the fridge can get quite hot) whereas the ASHP makes use of the heat for your home. The pump uses a refrigerant (antifreeze) that boils at -15* C so even when it's freezing cold outside, the heat pump can still work effectively. Trying to understand this bends my mind, so please don't expect a more technical explanation. This article by Which?[1] gives you more of an idea without trying to sell you something specific.

Suffice it to say, heating continues regardless of the weather, although when it's cold the ASHP does have to work harder. It uses electricity to run the compressor and pump but creates three times the amount of heat per kilowatt hour of electricity used. Modern ASHPs have a COP of 3:1 or even 4:1. There is also a seasonal coefficient of performance (SCOP) figure, which gives a year-long average so you can see how the unit functions throughout the different seasons.

All of this means that costs will be much lower than for standard electric heaters. To be fully environmentally sustainable you need to buy your electricity from a provider that specialises in renewables or create your own through solar (see below) or wind power.

Heat pumps are increasingly popular so there are a number of brands to choose from. They sit outside the house against the wall, within 30m of the house or on a flat roof, and are essentially a fan in a box about three times the size of an air conditioning machine. The machine links through into a hot water storage tank similar to the hot water tank with a gas boiler.

ASHPs can be fitted in flats as well as houses, although it will be a bit more difficult for a flat. One of the requirements is that the heat pump needs to be sited away from neighbours to avoid noise issues and this may not be so easy in tightly packed housing. The practical problems obviously get harder as the height of the building increases, but the units can be attached to the wall like an air conditioning unit, so it is certainly worth asking.

Common concerns

Many people on the forums voice similar concerns, and I was no exception, so let's look at them:

What about the noise?

Since our pump was to sit on top of the flat roof of the new extension, just above the back door, I was very concerned about the amount of noise in the garden and our new kitchen. Avid Facebook scrolling told me of people who were so worried they decided not to take the risk. In the end our provider took us to visit the recommended machine so we could actually hear it and that put our minds at rest.

The rhetoric claims that the noise is similar to that of a fridge and that you can easily have a normal conversation beside it. Sounds right, mind you we did get the one that professed to be the quietest on the market. The noise from ours would never stop a conversation – nowhere near. It's no more noisy than any other heating system.

ASHP on the roof above the main living area.

We spend most of our day directly beneath it, so on bitterly cold days I have noticed a very gentle thrum but I find it quite a comforting sound. On the vast majority of days, I don't notice it at all, inside or outside the house.

Will it save money?

Having had the ASHP for one year, we've been able to make a comparison of energy usage. We compared the year before we began the renovation, when we had gas central heating and used electricity for cooking, lighting, charging the car etc, with our first year of full use of the ASHP in the insulated house. We were amazed to discover that **we've saved three-quarters of the kilowatt hours used previously.** Interestingly, we have saved all the cost of the gas and now pay a similar amount to the previous cost of electricity, but now it's for everything. Given that prices change, we decided to stick with ratios and kilowatt hours and I expect the ratio to remain the same – the amount used for electricity in a gas-heated house now covers everything.

Will it deliver enough hot water?

Someone asked me this the other day and the question had never occurred to me. Which I guess tells you that it is delivering enough hot water – for us, anyway.

The ASHP heats the water up to 55*C which is lower than the normal 60*C of central heating levels. (However new building regulations mean that 55*C is the maximum flow temperature for any new heating systems.) In fact, 60*C is extremely hot when it comes to normal use and even 55*C will have to be reduced to around 40* C in a shower mixer. We are shower people and the main person who uses the bath is my little grandson and he doesn't need it to be full to the brim so it's working fine for him, too.

If there is a problem with hot water, I understand that the ASHP is not the issue – it's whether the hot water tank you have is large enough to hold the water you need. So if you like a very full bath, make sure you let your provider know so they can plan the system accordingly.

And what's this about Legionnaires' disease?

Now, this did give me pause for thought, but of course it's all been worked out so no cause for alarm.

Legionnaires' is a type of bacterium that thrives in warm water. If left unattended, it can cause headaches, coughs and even pneumonia over time. It's not a problem in traditional systems because the water is too hot. With an ASHP the water temperature of 55*C could be attractive to the bacteria. The simple answer is to raise the heat on a regular basis to above 60*C. This is achieved by having an immersion heater included in the system.

Our system raises the temperature overnight one day a week. I can't say I've ever noticed a difference in the water temperature on the following day, although I've read that some people can. The only interest we had in knowing when it was happening was to see if there was any difference in energy use. We haven't particularly noticed that, either.

———

It has to be cashmere

I was known for my scarves. The scarf holder in my wardrobe came close to pulling the door off its hinges, I have so many. They became a signature piece – I needed every colour you can think of so there would be at least one to match my outfit.

When younger, I was happy with wool and synthetic, but as the years piled on I just had to be warmer and anything scratchy was literally a pain in my neck. Until the day I discovered the wonderful, gentle touch of cashmere. On our sabbatical trip to Nepal, my first question was, "Where can I get top-quality cashmere?"

It sounds awful. What a princess!

It suddenly occurred to me the other day – it's so long since I wore a scarf. Is it retirement? Covid? No – I'm just not cold anymore, thanks to the air source heat pump, insulation, airtightness... In fact, if I put on a scarf these days, I'm peeling it off in minutes. It just shows how very cold our house was before the renovation. I would layer up in thermals, cashmere jumpers, hoodie and scarves just to come downstairs. Now I can dress normally and be comfortable all day. I can also be inside with no idea how cold the weather is outside.

So is an eco renovation worth it? Warm body, wardrobe doors no longer in peril and much lower energy usage. I rest my case.

———

Which ASHP did we go for?

In the end we went for the Mitsubishi 8.5KwH^2 heat pump. It has a good reputation and claimed to be the quietest on the market. But it all depends on the needs of your home, lifestyle and the amount of insulation and airtightness you have achieved. As your insulation increases, so the size of the required heat pump goes down.

This is one of those occasions when it's really important to find a reliable and honest provider – someone who will listen fully to your plans for the eco development of your house and take the time to understand what your needs will be. There are numerous calculations that go into the decision – relating to house size, energy efficiency, family requirements etc. I did my best to understand what was involved and how the decision about size of pump was made, but it really was beyond me, hence the need for a provider you can trust.

Take time to prepare for these discussions. For your provider to make an accurate assessment of your needs, they need a clear understanding of what you are going to put in place in detail, even down to the effectiveness of your loft hatch. If you don't provide this information, there's a risk you'll end up with a bigger heat pump than you need – which would mean greater expense, more energy usage over time and a machine that takes up more space for no better performance.

Ground source heat pump

A ground source heat pump (GSHP; also known as ground to water heat pump) works in a similar way to the ASHP but is slightly more consistent because the heat comes from the ground and is not weather dependent. A GSHP needs pipes laid horizontally underground over the area of a football pitch or vertically into deeply drilled bore holes, both drawing natural heat from the earth and transferring it to your heat pump. Like the ASHP it needs electricity to run, but whereas the ASHP has to work harder in cold weather, when you need heat most, the GSHP is more constant so it uses less electricity in winter. This makes the running costs lower overall.

The downside is that installation costs are much higher because significant machinery is required to drill the bore hole or dig up and lay the pipes over a wide area.

If you get on well with your neighbours and plan to stay in your home for a good length of time, the ability to share a bore hole might be interesting. Getting the drilling gear in place is the biggest cost with a GSHP so, once it's there,

HEATING AND SOLAR ENERGY

increasing the number of bore holes to feed more than one house is a relatively small cost. There would of course need to be clear agreements about joint responsibilities, but it might be worth looking into.

The same points apply when speaking with your builder and other providers. Be really clear about your plans for making the house environmentally sound so they can take this into account in their calculations.

———

To ASHP or not to ASHP

Despite our certainty about the ASHP, once we talked with people about what they'd done, I started to waver. There are so many opinions out there about what is right and it can be hard to find someone who actually has a heat pump to hear about real-time experience.

Being a cold body, reading about a steady but lower temperature gave me the collywobbles. I can hear the family chorusing "she hates being cold", coupled with my other favourite phrase "I'm glad I brought me coat." I even started to look up options for electric heating. I knew we had to give up on gas, but could I stand low temperatures? I just wasn't sure.

In the end it was the touchstone, our early decision about priorities, that carried the day. In my heart, I knew that the earth had to come first. I still wasn't totally convinced, but honestly the decision was already made. Once the pump was switched on (com-missioned), I spent too long checking the thermostat: was it warm enough? Could I feel the cold? Did we need to turn it up? I drove myself up the wall for a while.

And then I came to realise – this was fine. I hardly noticed anything happening, other than feeling cosy warm. I could see when the thermostat was turning the temperature down, but the room was already so nice, it made very little difference. The house had become the new version of 'me coat' – cosy, comforting and utterly reliable.

———

RADIATORS VERSUS UFH

Whether you've decided on a heat pump or traditional gas boiler, the next conversation is about radiators or underfloor heating (UFH). UFH is the recommended option, especially for an ASHP, but I have to admit I had a bit of a moan about it – I've spent a lot of time working in Scandinavia with swollen feet, especially in hot hotel bathrooms. But when we discovered that the heat pump works to a lower constant temperature, I was willing to think again.

However, there is one problem with UFH – it needs to be well insulated underneath to prevent loss of heat to the ground and it needs a good conductor above so the heat can come freely into the room. It works fine under wooden floors, laminates, tiles etc, but a carpet will hold the heat in – particularly significant for the lower temperature of a heat pump.

In the end we settled on a mixture of UFH and radiators. We have a wooden floor throughout the dining room and kitchen/family room with UFH, which works really well. However, we like carpet in the front room and upstairs so we stayed with radiators there.

Will the existing radiators work?

Because the ASHP central heating temperature is lower, the surface area of the radiators needs to be larger to get maximum warmth into the room. This is what we were told, so it's what we did.

When choosing these radiators you have to work out the amount of heat you require in a room given its size and level of insulation/airtightness. Your provider will use a specific formula to work out what size you need. A large room that is not well insulated will require a big radiator, or even two. There is only one design on the market at present and, honestly, it's not the most attractive thing I've ever seen. The style is pretty industrial, with a fan included in case you want to boost the heat when you get up in the morning. Also it's not cheap. So if you're happy with wooden floors, laminate or tiles with rugs, stick with UFH.

The bigger question is: did we need the large radiators? It's such a tough call – changing radiators means upheaval, so is best done all at once. The last thing you want is to have to rip everything up again. So we followed the norm. And in the concern about being cold, we even left in an existing radiator in the dining room alongside the UFH.

With the magic of hindsight we think the big radiators might have been overkill, given the level of insulation and airtightness we created. We use just one radiator (intermittently) upstairs plus the towel rail in the bathroom. Downstairs we haven't needed to use the old radiator we left in. The only one we can't be sure of is in the sitting room – no way to know if the old one would have worked, but we suspect it would have been fine.

What about rugs?

This was another one of those conundrums, with different people telling us different things. Received wisdom is that carpet or thick rugs over UFH will:

- block your heat – the rug/carpet will hold the heat between itself and the floor
- warp your wooden floor – as the heat builds up with nowhere to go, so the wood itself will be damaged.

What we could never get clear about – I guess because the ASHP is still relatively new – is whether lower heat in the UFH carried the same risks. Not many flooring people we spoke to understood the implications of the ASHP, so you need to ask around; talk with different people and see what you can find out. It's a judgement call that only you can make.

In the end we went for an engineered wood floor and found a much thinner rug to go on top of it. Where we have a much-loved rug, we just took out the underlay and crossed our fingers. So far so good – both rugs are working just fine.

SOLAR ENERGY

The ASHP makes heat from the air, which is brilliant, but it's still driven by electricity. So from a eco perspective the ideal is to generate your own power, becoming carbon neutral for heating.

Unless you have a huge plot of land and neighbours who won't object to a windmill, your most likely option for energy generation is a solar photovoltaic system (PV) i.e. solar panels on your roof. If you get these working, they will drive the heat pump and then... I was going to say 'you'll be cooking on gas', but I guess we need to find a more eco version of the old saying.

I'm afraid I can't explain how it actually works. If you want more technical details from a source that isn't trying to sell you something, this article[3] from the Centre for Alternative Technology might help.

When considering installing solar panels, you need to take into account a number of issues:

- direction your roof faces
- size and angle of your roof
- levels of shade
- DNO restrictions
- council restrictions.

Direction your roof faces

The ideal is a south-facing roof, so your panels will receive the sun at its most powerful for the longest time, allowing you to generate most energy. However, you can still install panels on rooftops with an east or west orientation and generate a reasonable amount. The morning sun will be reflected off an east-facing roof, whereas the afternoon and evening sun will reflect off a west-facing roof. Sadly if your roof faces north, solar probably won't make financial sense.

It is possible to install panels on the roof of a garage or a shed, as long as you can strengthen the roof enough to carry the weight. You can also put panels in your garden if you have enough space. The further they are away from the house, the more expensive the installation, although you do cut out the cost of scaffolding required for a roof installation.

Size and angle of your roof

It makes sense that the bigger your roof space the more panels you can install. We discovered that, although the sizes of ordinary panels don't vary much, it is possible to have bigger, more industrial-sized ones to make the most of the space you have.

The panels also need to be at a specific angle to make the most of the sun's rays – 35*C is the optimum – but they will work reasonably well between 10*C and 60*C. If you only have a flat roof, then you can still have panels as long as there is space for them to be angled towards the sun.

Levels of shade

The more shade that blocks the panel, the less energy you can produce. So if your house is surrounded by trees, you have a tough call to make. The importance of trees is so ingrained by now that it's hard to think of cutting them down for any reason. Removing one important environmental feature to put in another feels like robbing Peter to pay Paul.

However, these decisions are not restricted to solar. We all constantly weigh up where the most benefit lies, so refer back to your touchstone and the decision may become a little easier.

Distribution network operator (DNO) restrictions

The larger your roof, the more panels you can have – in theory. If the number you want is very large or if neighbours around you already have panels, you may encounter restrictions. An application will be made to the local distribution network operator (DNO) on your behalf to find out what is possible. They will consider whether the existing electrical connection from your house to the grid is suitable, as well as deciding whether the excess energy you generate might unbalance the grid.

Council restrictions

Generally, in the UK, solar panels are part of permitted development, so you don't need to have planning permission, but they do need to pass standard building regulations.

The only time you need to consider the planning rules is if you live in a conservation area or a listed building. However, new national policy allows for houses in conservation areas to have solar panels, unless the panels protrude above the highest part of the roof or if the house is on a highway.

Since neither of those restrictions apply to us, this news made it possible for us to go ahead with solar so we were delighted. It would be difficult for any council to justify refusing eco developments just because they don't look nice when the earth is in such a state.

———

We're feeding the grid!

It's our new early morning call. Our roof isn't the best for solar and our most productive time is during the morning. So that little emblem on the smart meter that means the grid is benefitting is the sign to put on the dishwasher, sort out the dirty washing, plug in the car – whatever we've been saving for the sunshine. It's such a lovely feeling to know I'm cooking or charging my laptop for 'free'.

Our house roof faces east–west, so we have five panels on the east-facing roof and three on the west face. Neither is optimal, but we can get about 75% of an average south-facing output and that's not to be sniffed at. I admit I do suffer from 'array envy'. I look at large houses that clearly face south with a vast number of panels and I want the same. I also get pretty self-righteous when I see empty roofs – "Look at that fabulous roof and not a solar panel in sight!" Not my best feature, but it has inspired us to think about re-ordering the shed in our garden to provide a solar roof.

(I'll be writing about our progress on my blog: https://ecorenovationhome.com)

Out of all the work we've had done, I was surprised that this was the most exciting. Taking what nature provides and using it for good feels very special. My best day of all is a sunny, windy day – washing courtesy of the sun and drying courtesy of the wind. I can be a right Lucy Leek! (Age-related reference - apologies. All you need to know is that "Lucy Leek loved lather!")[4]

————

Whether or not to have a battery

This is a big question – does the value of storing the excess energy your PV panels produce justify the environmental impact of producing a battery? This Centre for Sustainable Energy article[5] is pretty comprehensive about the use of batteries, although not much about the eco impact of their manufacture.

If you have an electric vehicle, you may be able to do without a fixed battery in the house and simply use the one in your car. Some energy suppliers have the technology to feed electricity back to the house i.e. bi-directional charging. It is also possible to programme some car chargers to use energy from solar when it is available. Technology is constantly changing in this area so if a battery is of interest, go exploring and see what you can find.[6]

Solar water heating

If you're like me, you'll have spotted this as you travel around but not understood what it was. These panels are much smaller and are often in isolation on a roof. When you look closely you can see that the panel is made up of pipes. This is direct water heating with the water picking up the heat from the sun. You can find out more about how it works online[7].

Generally, a solar water heating system can produce between 40% and 70% of the hot water needed by an average family of four annually, so worth consideration.

SUMMARY

- There are different options for heating. In terms of being eco-friendly and available, heat pumps - air source and ground source - come well up the list.
- Heat pumps work at a lower temperature so work best when coupled with increased insulation and airtightness.
- Ground source is more consistent throughout the year but more expensive to install; air source needs to work a little harder during the winter months. Both are very efficient when part of a complete eco set up.
- Underfloor heating is the preferred option with a heat pump. If you prefer radiators, they may need to be larger to give a bigger surface area.
- You will need lighter rugs to avoid blocking heat from the UFH.
- Solar panels need a roof that faces south for the best output; south-east or south-west gives 'good enough' output.

- You need an unshaded roof and the ability to set the panels at an angle of 20–50 degrees so they can catch the sun.
- Solar panels can be put up under permitted development and according to building regulations. You need to check this if you are in a listed building or a conservation area.

For photographs of the ASHP, solar panels etc go to my blog: www.ecorenovationhome.com

---

1. http://www.which.co.uk/reviews/ground-and-air-source-heat-pumps/article/air-source-heat-pumps-explained-al5MC4f773Zq
2. https://les.mitsubishielectric.co.uk/products/residential-heating/outdoor
3. https://cat.org.uk/info-resources/free-information-service/energy/solar-photovoltaic
4. https://countryhouselibrary.co.uk/products/ladybird-the-garden-gang-lucy-leek-and-bertie-brussels-sprout-by-jayne-fisher-1979
5. https://www.cse.org.uk/advice/renewable-energy/battery-storage
6. https://www.fortum.com/products-and-services/fortum-battery-solutions/battery-related-news
7. http://www.energy.gov/energysaver/solar-water-heaters

CHAPTER 12
WINDOWS AND DOORS

"How do you manage with single-glazed windows in your cold, damp country?" This was the reaction of my Swedish friends after flat-hunting in London with their daughter. Used to triple glazing as standard, they found it hard to believe we could be so badly organised.

And they really do have a point. What are we doing still having such poor-quality windows when the cost of energy is skyrocketing and we have a climate crisis?

I know they were looking at rental properties, which are often less well cared for, but I still hear of homeowners who don't see glazing as an issue. I think we are so used to draughts and cold windows that it doesn't occur to us because we just turn up the central heating. In reality a good-quality double or triple-glazed window is worth its weight in gold, with the comfort and warmth it provides more than compensating for the outlay.

There are a number of different options for improving the efficiency of windows and doors:

- double glazing
- secondary glazing
- triple glazing
- window repair
- windowpane replacement.

A lot depends on the style of your house. Having an old Victorian end-of-terrace house means we have traditional sash windows at the front. The rest of our windows have all been replaced, but we do feel very attached to those last bits of Victorian style.

Living in modern houses makes for an easier choice. You probably started with double glazing so the choice was already made, but whether it is still effective or as energy efficient as it could be is another matter – that will depend on the age of your building.

In even older houses – pre-Victorian – the question can be a lot more complex. If your property is listed you'll be limited by what is allowed, although there will still be ways around it. You don't have to live in a beautiful but draughty old place for ever.

U VALUE

When you talk to providers about glazing they will tell you about the U value of the products you're considering. You can read more about U values in chapter 7 but, in short, the U value tells you how efficient your window will be by measuring the heat lost through the single, double or triple panes. The lower the number, the less heat lost. On average, U values are:

- single glazing – 5.6 W/m^{2}K
- old double glazing – 2.8 W/m^{2}K
- new double glazing – 1.2 W/m^{2}K
- triple glazing – 0.8-0.6 W/m^{2}K.

Another way of understanding this is that one-fifth of the heat lost from a home can be due to old single-glazed windows. Modern double glazing should be three times better, with triple glazing five times better[1]. I think that's called a 'no-brainer'.

Single glazing

Before we understood about climate and environment, we thought single glazing was fine. I remember living with the original metal-framed windows. Not sure they'd have been real Crittall ones in a Wolverhampton council house, but it was the same impact – b****y cold! Condensation dripping, mould growing and cold air circulating everywhere. Maybe this is why my parents taught me to sleep with the windows open at night – not doing this would have left puddles on the windowsill.

Single glazing is still remarkably common, not to mention metal windows, which are even worse. It's always a balance – will the cost to replace them be more than the cost of lost heat? As energy goes up – and up – then the equation may well begin to tip firmly in the direction of new windows.

Double glazing

We're on very familiar territory with this. So familiar, I realise I haven't heard a joke about double-glazing salesmen for years. That must be a relief to all concerned.

There are numerous types of double glazing[2], but I don't think I have to tell you that. Whatever the type, there are a number of benefits:

- keeps warm air in, improving your insulation, so fewer draughts and cheaper heating bills
- keeps external noise out and your noise in

- stops condensation on the glass by providing a warm inner layer
- improves security – more difficult to break into a double layer of glass.

Double glazing in and of itself is going to add value from a climate perspective, saving energy and increasing the value of your property. However, it doesn't last forever – and there are constant advancements that make the product increasingly effective, so do keep an eye on the efficiency of what you have.

A thermal imaging camera[3] will show you where heat loss is higher – for example, where poor sealing of the window into its frame allows cold air to infiltrate. It can't tell you how much air you're losing, but it is a huge help in identifying the weak spots where action needs to be taken. You can hire one, sometimes for free, and you'll learn so much about the state of your home (see chapter 7).

Triple glazing

Given the comments of my Swedish friends, we had to go and at least look at triple glazing. What I learned from that experience is:

- Triple glazing has the same benefits as double glazing, only more so, and can be up to 40% more efficient. The extra layer of glass, air and gas provides superior insulation and a greater reduction in sound. Condensation doesn't even come into the equation.
- The best high-performance windows will be a composite of wood and aluminium or PVC and aluminium.
- Triple-glazed windows feel very robust and solid, which gives a pleasing sense of security.

- The difference in price is less than expected, especially taking into account the quality of the end product and, as ever, there are deals to be done.

If you are going for a thorough eco renovation, then you're more likely to get Passivhaus-level expertise from a reputable triple-glazing company, which can be very helpful. Do let them know at the outset that this is the standard you expect. This should mean they take good care over the fit and maintenance of the airtightness line.

———

How much are we willing to spend?

As we drove towards our first visit to a glazing specialist, we pondered the question together – how much more are we willing to pay for triple glazing? We both really wanted it – it felt right for the standard of eco we were aiming for. But we did need to think about budget.

As we drove away, we were both already committed – not least because of the quality of the product. Even to my novice eye, the windows were beautifully engineered. The performance was excellent and the frames would certainly see me out. We also discovered that the price difference for all that was only about 20% more than double glazed. I've seen recently the offer of triple for the price of double, so it's well worth looking around.

I know that in the middle of a renovation 20% can be quite a lot. My logic was that we could delay other costs – such as the interior design elements – but windows had to go in now. If they were high quality, it would be a good 50–60 years before they'd need replacing, so overall cost would be very low and waste even lower. So it felt worth a reshuffle of the budget to make it possible and fitted well with Passivhaus[4] principles, i.e. go for the best whenever you can.

It's not just the windows – it's the fit

There are two aspects to be aware of when getting new windows: one is the window itself, described and evaluated in websites and advertising blurb. The second is how well the window fits into the space in the wall. I talked about this a little in chapter 8 on airtightness for obvious reasons – any gaps will break the airtightness line and leave you with draughts, which is galling after all the work of finding the right materials and provider.

If you're replacing windows in your existing home, the position of the window in the wall space will already have been decided. If you are adding an extension, it's worth finding out ahead of time from your builder or architect exactly how they need to be fitted in case there is a question at the time. You don't want to create a thermal bridge, so the window needs to sit behind the brick or the outer facing, overlapping with the insulation. Unfortunately, this wasn't done well for us and we had to make do, filling in the gaps left by the wrong positioning. So get professional advice as soon as possible and make sure you have experts on site when the windows go in – it will greatly reduce your frustration.

Take time in choosing a provider and ask for recommendations to make sure you have someone who will do a really good job. It's also a good idea to borrow a thermal imaging camera so you or a professional can check on the fit before you pay the final bill.

Double versus triple glazing

Given the comparative U values, it may seem that double glazing is more than good enough – after all, from a 5.6 W/m^2k single-glazed window to a new double-glazed window of 1.2 W/m^2k is a major difference. However, when you take into account that walls are rated at 0.18 W/m^2k it's clear that even double glazing has a long way to go and triple starts to look more inviting.

If your budget is limited and an overall 20% extra is too much, you could put triple glazing on the north side of your house – the coldest side. Then follow up with the east and west sides when you can afford it.

We settled for Internorm[5] windows with a U value of 0.6 and, I have to say, I take pleasure in them every day!

Improving the U value

There are two options that help to improve the U value:

- **Gases held between the layers** – high-performance windows hold a noble (inert) gas in between the layers of glazing; it is highly stable, with extremely low reaction rates. The molecules of the noble gases (argon, krypton or xenon) are at greater distance from each other than molecules of heavier gases, so the transmission of heat is more difficult, giving them a lower heat conductivity than air. (Am I the only one thinking superhero now? Love the idea of a noble gas!)
- **Low emissivity coating or e-coating** – this covers the glass to reduce the amount of

ultraviolet/infrared light that passes through the glass as heat without affecting the visible light. It's a microscopically thin, transparent coating that reflects the heat back into the room.

Solar gain – if your house faces south with plenty of access to the sun, a decision will need to be made about the impact of summer, not to mention future climate scenarios. This is a matter for your architect, so make sure it's included in your initial design/plan and that issues such as shade and over-heating are addressed from the outset. Your architect will then be able to help with decisions about e-coating or the type of glazing you need to maintain any warmth from the sun as well as cutting out cold and draughts.

Trickle vents – finally there is the issue of the trickle vent, a small grid at the top of the window to allow an exchange of air. For more about this, read chapter 10 on ventilation. In summary, there are more energy-efficient ways of ensuring clean air without losing all the warmth you've spent so much time creating.

Secondary glazing

This is ideal for older houses where you have to retain the style but need to do something about cold single glazing. Secondary is a cheaper option, although only half as effective as double glazing.

The process adds a whole new glass window that slides, tilts or lifts out completely, within the same window frame. The depth of the gap can be adapted to suit, including making the gap bigger if noise reduction is required. It's important to make sure that the secondary windows fit well into their frames, so they close tight and reduce draughts.

If you do go for secondary glazing, make sure the installer creates a good airtight seal. Without this you might get condensation on the cold surface of your outside window as warm air from the room passes through a leaky seal.

Repair of existing glass panes

I had no idea this was possible so I was delighted to come across a company that focused entirely on repairing and renovating original wooden sash windows. It was a no-brainer for us – just what we needed to keep our charming wooden Victorian sashes. A whole new inner window was made, then slotted into the refurbished window surround. No one would be any the wiser from the outside, but the new unit is double glazed. Given the restriction of the existing window sizes it hasn't got the biggest double-glazing gap, but it's significantly better than it was. Also, the renovation included draught insulation brushes to make them more airtight.

This is a very real option nowadays if you live in a listed building, since conservation officers are increasingly allowing slimline double glazing, which is great!

So consult the internet and see if you can find an equivalent business in your area. Even if you decide to go for new windows in the end, it's well worth considering this as an option and it might be just what you are looking for.

Old houses and their windows

Double and triple glazing are no-brainers, unless you live in a very old house or in a listed building where there are limits on what you can change externally. We went to visit a friend recently in the most beautiful old house with floor-to-ceiling windows – the rooms were stunning and decorated with real style. Only problem – as soon as I walked into the room I could feel cold air emanating from the windows. It must cost a fortune to heat.

Yet there are ways to do it. We could always have changed our sash windows for modern double glazing but it would really change the look of the house, so when we first moved in 40 years ago, we went for secondary glazing. Initially it was for sound privacy – I was working from home as a psychotherapist at the time and wanted confidentiality / didn't want to scare the neighbours. However, I soon realised that it was a real improvement in heat retention. Over the years I've wondered how effective the secondary was but never did anything about it until the recent retrofit.

It didn't make sense to dump the old secondary, so we decided to reinstate it over the newly refurbished sashes – belt and braces – why not? Testing it all out with the thermal imaging camera showed us that it was still doing a good job, so now we have a version of 'triple' glaze in the front room, too.

———

DOORS

There isn't that much difference between doors and windows in terms of glazing:

- Fit is super important – we all know the impact of a draughty door and letterbox.

- Safety glass may be important – especially if you have a small, energetic youngster around the place, as we do.
- Bifolds look amazing, but they must be fitted perfectly. Working with such large pieces of glass and additional fixings is a delicate issue and they must be totally right, otherwise there is a risk of air leakage.
- The sills of any door are part of the mechanism, so treat them carefully. Standing on them or dragging heavy objects across them may dislodge something important. (We didn't know this and managed to dislodge the rubber seal by standing on it and that led to air leakage.)
- You will only get the full seal on the door when you lift the handle up to 'lock' it in position from an airtightness perspective. So getting in the habit of lifting the handle each time is a real help.

Shutting off a cold space

If you have a cold space that you can't heat efficiently, one option is to put in a door and close it off from the rest of the house – for example, a cold utility room, a cloakroom, a hallway. Putting in a solid or double-glazed door is a very effective way of shutting out the cold.

We did this with a conservatory-style hallway. Without a complete rebuild, there was little we could do to insulate it, and we wanted to keep the light from the hall coming into the dark dining room. Our idea was to install a double-glazed Crittall-style door. Not only does it look good, but it is also extremely effective in keeping the cold out. So now it's like going from outside to inside, so great is the temperature difference.

Making sure a door closes automatically is also a good investment. You can buy a door spring in any DIY store and, once it's installed, it will make sure you keep the heat in the room at all times.

BE PREPARED

It's only a window/door, for heaven's sake – or so I thought. Like much of deciding on building options, my experience of talking glazing was that I quickly became overwhelmed and just wanted it to be finished so I could go home. However, I soon learned that if I took a bit of time to make sure I understood the terminology then I would have a much clearer, more useful conversation. It took less time and I had the chance of a much better outcome in the end.

SUMMARY

- Investing in double, triple or secondary glazing can make a big difference to heating bills.
- Triple glazing can be up to 40% more efficient than double glazing and only approximately 20% more expensive.
- It's vital to find a provider who will fit the windows well because additional heat can be lost through an ill-fitting frame.
- You can improve the U value (effectiveness measure) through the addition of a noble gas in the gap between the panes – e.g. argon, krypton.
- Doors carry all the same issues as windows. In addition, you need to take care of the frame and sills, because they can cause a lack of airtightness over quite a large area.
- Triple- or double-glazed doors need to be 'locked in' – i.e. the door handle needs to be lifted into place to ensure full airtightness.

1. https://cat.org.uk/info-resources/free-information-service/eco-renovation/windows/
2. https://energysavingtrust.org.uk/advice/windows-and-doors
3. https://sustainablestalbans.org/thermal-imaging
4. https://www.passivhaustrust.org.uk
5. https://uk.internorm.com

CHAPTER 13
APPLIANCES

Building a kitchen extension requires a new kitchen. Now we're getting to the lovely stuff! The chance to have all the cupboard space you need, not to mention new appliances.

For us, the renovation to the kitchen was so major that nothing from before was going to fit. And since I'm an avid cook, I took the opportunity to finally have the kitchen I'd always wanted, together with all the bits and pieces that would make life easy. However, we still wanted to maintain the eco-friendly nature of the house, so that meant looking for the most energy-efficient appliances we could find.

ENERGY RATING

At the time, the rating[1] ranged from A+++ down to D. Now it has all changed and goes from A to G. It's well worth taking the time to find out more about the energy efficiency of the machines you need. The payback will come on those days when you need everything running at once but you don't want a massive bill at the end of it.

I've taken a look at the new ratings. There seem to be variations in explanation according to the machine, so it will take study to find what you need. It may be that a higher rating is also a higher cost but remember to set that against lower energy bills in the future and generally greater efficiency.

———

This is my moment!

A good thing about backing down from an entrenched position — e.g. I don't want this renovation work to happen — is the credit it brings with it. John was determined that I would have the kitchen of my dreams. Of course, he wasn't unaware that this would also mean more goodies to eat and less work for him. He's not stupid!

I thought I didn't have many specific needs, but once I got going, there was a lot I really wanted. A combi steam oven was high on the list. A hot water tap followed quickly behind — less clutter on the worktop and heating only the water we needed — plus the extractor fan located in an induction hob — easy to clean, better energy-wise and less chance of hitting my head on the cooker hood.

For us, this meant primarily Miele — best energy rating I could find for ovens, freezer, warming drawer. Fridge had to be Liebherr (but apparently they make Miele fridges) and the only fail was the washing machine. To have it integrated, I had to go to A++ in Bosch.

The important thing for me is that when I have them running, we see next to no change on the smart meter. So they really are using small amounts of energy. I've *learned not to follow recipes where the first instruction is to light the oven, because it only takes mine a few minutes to heat up to even 225*C.*

Finally – nothing to do with energy ratings – if you have the chance to lift your dishwasher up to waist height, do it. John was determined. I thought it was ridiculous (meant it was situated away from the sink) but now I know it to be a masterful decision. No more moaning about whose turn it is to empty the crocks – it's so easy, it's almost a pleasure!

SUMMARY

- Continue being eco-friendly as you choose appliances.
- Consult the energy rating of each item – it may cost a little more, but it will use less energy over many years.
- Using less energy means different ways of working, so think before following your old patterns.
- Think more widely as you design your kitchen – new thinking can be life-changing.

---

1. https://energysavingtrust.org.uk/advice/home-appliances/

CHAPTER 14
DÉCOR

Once the major building work is done, then it's on to the décor. So exciting – the final part of making the house inviting and comfortable. This is familiar territory. You've been imagining how each room will look since before the work began, so it's tempting to just dive in and forget about being eco.

Questions to ask:

- Paintwork – will we use eco paint or standard options?
- Flooring – sustainable or non-biodegradable?
- Lighting – LED or halogen?
- Packaging of new items?
- Quality or quantity?

PAINTWORK

I'd love to tell you that we'd done extensive research into the best paint to use with breathable materials – but sadly I can't. We were blessed with a decorator who was fascinated by what we were doing and determined to check out the best paint for the job. It was through his research that we found breathable paint.

Paint is the final layer of the breathable unit on both sides of the wall – from external paintwork through to the lime plaster, the paintwork completes the job. It is an essential element of breathability that ensures moisture can move freely through the wall, managing condensation in the room.

Any paint that contains vinyl, acrylic, oils or plastics isn't breathable, so will trap moisture beneath the surface, causing mould build-up or even blowing the paint off entirely – something I'm sure we've all seen somewhere over the years. The great advantage of breathable paint is that it won't trap moisture, so no risk your paintwork will end up flaking.

Choosing an eco-friendly paint is quite a minefield, the language used by manufacturers can be confusing, and as paint is made from a number of ingredients it's difficult to trace what they all are and where they have come from. The main things to check are:

- Does the paint contain VOCs (volatile organic compounds). If you've ever had a headache after painting a room without enough ventilation that's the VOCs at work. It is difficult to produce paint without them so choose paint with the lowest VOC content that you can.
- Does the paint contain titanium dioxide? This gives paint its brightness, and many colours can't be produced without it. Titanium dioxide is extremely energy- and resource-intensive to produce and results in a lot of waste. Try to choose a paint with as low a titanium dioxide content as possible. Earthborn[1] are very transparent about which of their colours do and don't contain this element.

If you are doing the painting yourself think about how you'll dispose[2] of the waste. Do not pour paint down the sink and clean as much paint as possible from your brushes and rollers before washing them. Even eco paints contribute to water pollution.

If you're using paint made from a natural material like lime, once it's dry you can compost it. Conventional paint, once dried, needs to go to a paint collection point, which is probably at your local recycling centre. If you have a lot of liquid paint left over then save it for touch-ups, or donate it to an organisation like Community RePaint[3].

The painting adventure

I'd never heard about Earthborn until our painter Harry told me about it. Thank heavens for his perfectionism! I just hadn't thought of paint as part of the equation. For so many years, we just went to B&Q and looked for the colour we wanted. Thoughts about the paint itself never entered my mind – just cost and whether I wanted to risk a mixed paint or not.

There are a few makes that include breathable products in their range. Mostly you have to order in advance, so don't expect instant access. Also it's true that the range is smaller – but given the enormous range of mixed paints available these days that's hardly surprising. I understand they go on in much the same way, so it's no more or less of a job.

We did a bit of manoeuvring in the kitchen. We have one wall – the outside wall behind the sink – where we reverted to standard kitchen paint. Because this is a relatively new wall – two extensions ago – it's a modern cavity wall. It's also one of only two places where we used PIR - we'd made a mistake with kitchen measurements and had to reduce the thickness of insulation. The thin PIR gave us both insulation and space – and it allowed us to have kitchen paint that can be scrubbed. And given I'm both an avid and pretty untidy cook, this was a distinct advantage.

Harry was amazing. He went to a specialist paint shop and had them match up the Earthborn colour on the adjoining lime wall with a paint for the PIR wall. There is actually a hair's breadth of difference in colour that we could all see at the time, but now have forgotten completely. One of those tiny bits of minutiae that felt huge at the time and now seems absurd with the benefit of hindsight.

FLOORING

When considering what you want to put on your floor there are a number of factors to take into account, not least of which is design and how you want the room to look. Through all that dust and mess, you've probably had wonderful images of thick carpets, fabulous wood, shiny tiles – whatever suits your style.

If you're also thinking eco, then you'll be looking for something made from renewable material that's been sustainably harvested with minimal damage to the environment, doesn't involve chemicals in production and will biodegrade at the end of its life rather than sit around in landfill forever. Not much!

From a day-to-day perspective you want something that will still look good in 10 or 20 years, can take a beating from family/friends/parties, is easy to keep clean and can stand getting wet if the worst happens.

Then there are specific needs. For example, if you're going for an ASHP and underfloor heating then you do need to consider the combined impact on your floor. Certain types of flooring are designed with UFH in mind – it can sit on top of hot pipes without warping or being damaged. It also needs to be of a material that will allow maximum heat into the room – after all, having a warm, cosy house is what this is all about.

Marmoleum

I'd never heard of this until we started hunting for flooring. Turns out it's one of the most eco-friendly floors you can buy. It's made from 97% raw materials, 72% of which are rapidly renewable and 43% is recycled content. It is 100% biodegradable, made in UK factories, powered by 100% renewable electricity and contains zero nasties. Hard to compete with that! It's perfect for areas that take a beating – hallways, kitchens, bathrooms. No problems with it getting wet and easy to clean. It's definitely worth looking at.

Wood floors

This has got to be a good option as long as the timber is from a sustainable source. Look for the Forest Stewardship Council[4] certification – then you know the wood is all it is said to be. Producers have to comply with specific guidelines about how the forest has been managed with regard to biodiversity, how the wood is harvested and replaced, guaranteed sources and valid use of reclaimed materials – in fact, top-notch eco credentials all along the chain of production.

Solid wood will last – our floorboards are solid wood from 1900 and still in perfect shape – and it can be sanded to spruce it up when needed. (Our daughter sanded her bedroom floor in her teenage years and it looked great.) The downside is that it can be susceptible to humidity and damp, so is a bit risky in kitchens and bathrooms. Not to mention the fact that it can be extremely expensive, so it will depend on the health of your budget by the time you reach the floor stage.

Engineered wood looks the same as solid wood, but it is actually made of high-quality plywood with a single wood plank glued to it. Whether it can be refinished or not (sanded down and revarnished) will depend on the thickness of the top layer of wood.

Both forms of wooden floor need a lacquer of some sort to act as a barrier to damp and moisture. Without it there's a risk of the wood warping. What sort of lacquer you use is your choice. They can vary in levels of polish/shine and colour. So a pale wood can be varnished to look like a different wood altogether.

Another choice is how to fix the floor down. A solid wood floor can only be nailed. With an engineered wood floor it will depend to some degree on the existing underlying floor – whether it's concrete or a suspended floor. You can either glue or nail it down or float it over an underlay. In terms of sustainability, how you lay it will make a difference to whether it can be reused when you're ready for a change. If a floor is glued, then it's impossible to lift it without significant damage, in which case it's headed for the tip. If it's tongue and groove, it can be lifted and passed on.

———

A new home for the floated floor

The engineered wood floor in our old dining room and kitchen had done great service. The only mark was a small, but significant scratch from the day after it was laid. Unpacking a precious piece of furniture after our last renovation, we dragged the crate the last few inches – turned out to be a big mistake... huge!

John was keen to keep the floor and reuse it in the new kitchen but we'd need extra planks. I did my very best to order more (honestly, I did) but the truth was I'd never liked it. It was far too grainy and 'busy' for my liking.

Discovering the company had gone out of business was a relief and I finally owned up to wanting a new one. The compromise was that I'd find the wood a new home. There was also the laminate floor in our old conservatory, which was about to be removed by the builders, so I made my first foray onto Facebook Marketplace. The laminate went really quickly. Perfect, really – it built my confidence in rehoming and I was soon the queen of recycling (see chapter 15). The wooden floor took a little longer, but patience was rewarded. It went to someone who was running out of budget and also wasn't quite ready to take it all. She paid half the money, took the amount she needed straight away and returned when we were able to lift the final planks of wood.

Once John realised I'd lived with a floor I didn't like for so long, he was keen to find exactly the right one and he could feel OK because the old one wasn't going to waste.

It was all made possible by the fact that the floor was floated, rather than nailed or glued. So now we have the most beautiful floor – floated again – and I couldn't be more delighted!

Cork flooring

I remember this from the seventies – it was very cool to have cork in the kitchen. Nowadays, cork is known as an eco-friendly solution because it's made from organic and renewable materials. It's sustainable, versatile and beautiful. It's also really nice to live with – warm on the feet and quiet. It's made from the bark of the cork tree, which will be replenished within 10 years, so can be harvested again. The trees live on for up to 500 years – so it's challenging to be more sustainable than that.

However, there are downsides to cork: because it's such a good insulator it's not suitable for UFH. It's also quite soft, so is easily damaged; and you need to reapply the protective lacquer to maintain the water-resistant seal (just as you do with solid wood). If it gets very wet it will swell.

Bamboo

Bamboo is quite a new option and very eco-friendly because of the speed of growth. It's a grass and reaches maturity in a quarter of the time of a hardwood tree – two to three feet a day in its youth. You can float it or glue it down and some versions can be used over UFH. If you need a particularly durable floor, there is woven bamboo, which claims to be harder than hardwood.

The downside is that it can't be used in bathrooms or where there is excessive water and it can scratch if something is dragged across it.

There isn't much written about cork and bamboo other than on company sites. However, I did find a very detailed blog[5] if you want to go exploring.

Sisal, jute and Tencel

These are all alternatives to carpet with varying degrees of comfort, softness and durability – certainly worth considering if they fit with your style. You can find out more online[6].

Vinyl flooring

Luxury Vinyl Tile (LVT) can be made to look like wood or stone. It is made up of a series of layers, flexible and thin enough to cut through with a knife and is highly durable, suitable for areas of high usage. Vinyl flooring comes in different levels of quality from very expensive to cheap and cheerful.

Sadly vinyl is not eco-friendly. It is made from non-renewable resources (plastic), its production releases pollutants into the air, water and land, it can emit VOCs once installed and both floor and adhesives will emit harmful toxins should there be a fire. Oh, and it won't biodegrade at the end of its life.

If this is really what you want, then look into it thoroughly. Manufacturers understand that more people care about the environment these days so they do their best to please. On closer inspection, you may find that environmental credentials link primarily to packaging, energy use and recycling – all of which is laudable, but what isn't talked about is the raw materials used and the impact of manufacture.

LIGHTING

The main question when it comes to lighting is the light bulbs a shade can manage. Don't make the same mistake I did and assume that all shades will take LED bulbs. It's hard to believe that halogen bulbs are still in use, but they really are. So please do check the shade fully before you pay your money.

SOFT FURNISHINGS

All these eco questions really are of our time. When I was a kid in the 1950s there were few non-eco choices. We still made our curtains and the bolts of cloth in the haberdashers were natural fibres. But as I grew up and polyester made its debut, this all changed. Now it's hard to find natural fibres, as we discovered when talking with the person who was going to make new curtains for us.

I've been delighted with the response from providers when asked to think eco on our behalf and Nicola was no exception. She worked really hard to find us new or recycled natural fibres and, as a result of her dedication, we were able to choose from a reasonable range. Yet, just as with the paint, we had to expect our choices to be more limited, although I hope by the time you get there businesses will be catching on and stepping up their game.

So now we have a very elegant curtain beside our Crittall-style door that hasn't had a big environmental cost. Take it on as an adventure and a challenge and you'll be amazed what you can find.

KITCHEN

We'd had our last kitchen for 25 years and it was in great shape. Given the original space was much smaller than we have now, there was no way to reuse it, even though we'd have been happy to do so.

That statement was certainly true before we went to see kitchen providers and realised what was available 25 years on. As an avid cook, the drawers, larder cupboards and fabulous appliances were amazing – I was in heaven! But we still wanted to talk about the construction – would a new kitchen be robust enough for another 25 years? As my sister would say: this kitchen needed to 'see me out'. It'll be for the next owners to start again, not me.

Finally we went for German construction – a Häcker[7] kitchen – that has very good eco credentials, including having won many environmental and health protection awards. I was also very pleased to hear that they'd thought about wrapping and were using primarily cardboard, and it would all be taken away by the kitchen company and recycled.

There will be other kitchen producers that have such strong eco leanings; you just need to make that a question early on. If you fall in love with a kitchen before asking about being eco it will be much harder to move on, so be safe and make this one of your first considerations.

As we looked around, I soon realised that we could get most of what we wanted from any kitchen manufacturer. In fact there is little to choose between them in terms of design and special features. So what you're excited about from one producer will probably be just as easy to get from another, which means you can focus on the efficiency and attitude of your provider and the eco credentials.

And don't forget the appliances – see chapter 13 – because they are big energy users on a day-to-day basis.

BATHROOM

By the time you get to choosing bathroom fittings you'll either be heaving a sigh of relief because you're onto familiar territory or – like me – happy to say yes to anything just to be finished. However, we can still think eco:

- metal, stone, ceramics and porcelain are all more durable than plastic
- a low flow or dual flush toilet will help reduce your water usage

- a bidet or bidet toilet will cut down on toilet paper usage – food for thought!
- a shower that aerates the water means you use less and don't notice the difference
- a smart shower connects to an app and tells you how much water you've used.

If you are going for a breathable construction don't forget to check your eco-paint can be used in a bathroom. You may need to seal it with a protective glaze (make sure this is breathable too). And do remember to check that your tiling grout is breathable.

Here's an interesting one: a very trendy alternative option to tiles is Tadelakt[8] – a traditional Moroccan waterproof plaster. It is applied in one seamless layer, meaning no need for tiles or grouting, and making it ideal for a wet room. It can be tinted to colour it, meaning there is no need to paint on top. Fascinating.

PACKAGING

The final piece in terms of décor is to consider how your new goodies will be packaged. It's easier these days to get items wrapped in brown paper and cardboard, but when it comes to delicate wares like lights it is almost certain to be polystyrene and bubble wrap. So then the challenge is on to find a way to either recycle or reuse (see Chapter 15).

I would encourage you to ask the question. I always make a point of it when I'm buying a big-ticket item. It's unlikely to make a difference at the time, but if we all keep asking they may finally get the message.

And if all else fails, you can always put your surplus bubble wrap up on Freegle. Anyone moving house or packing to go to college will be grateful for it and at least it will get used more than once.

SUMMARY

- Paint is an important part of your breathability planning. It provides the final breathable layer inside and outside.
- There are a number of options for sustainable flooring. Go online and explore, making sure to dig into eco credentials.
- Make sure any lighting you buy can use LED bulbs.
- Soft furnishings can still be eco-friendly if you take time to research and the final products will be lovely.
- Most kitchen companies can provide what you need in terms of cupboards, drawers, units etc. Eco credentials are a real differentiator now and give a clue to the thought that has gone into the product. Ask early on so you can be sure to fall in love with a good one.
- Packaging can be a real trial. Ask how big items will be packed and, if all else fails, put plastic packaging on Freegle for people about to move and make sure it gets well used.

1. https://earthbornpaints.co.uk
2. https://www.diy.com/ideas-advice/how-to-recycle-paint-paint-cans/PROD_npcart_100261.art
3. https://communityrepaint.org.uk
4. https://fsc.org/en/certification-body-accreditation
5. http://www.ambientbp.com/blog/examining-the-effects-of-bamboo-hardwood-and-cork-flooring-on-humanitys-carbon-footprint
6. http://www.livingetc.com/advice/eco-flooring
7. https://about.haecker-kuechen.com/en/sustainability/ecology
8. https://tadelakt.co.uk/12-reasons-to-use-tadelakt-in-your-bathroom/

CHAPTER 15
RECYCLING

I actually enjoyed this part of the process. It's amazing how many lovely people you meet when seeking homes for your unwanted belongings.

It makes no sense to do an eco renovation, then dump loads of perfectly good stuff in the skip. An important part of our touchstone was to make sure we weren't littering the earth with our cast-offs. Instead we set out to find the person who would really like what we had and would enjoy giving it a home. And we managed remarkably well – only had to dump a bit of building stuff in the end.

A particular source of irritation that I can guarantee you'll have to deal with is the huge plastic weave bags that come with deliveries from builders' merchants. They are really strong bags, but never taken back for reuse and most are just dumped on the skip, ready to sit on the earth for hundreds of years. One option is to list them on gardening sites – they are perfect for collecting compost, weeds etc and they hold masses. They're a great example of the need to get inventive to avoid becoming an 'eco polluter'.

WHERE TO ADVERTISE

The habitual first port of call for most of us is the charity shop. Given we were doing all this in lockdown, that wasn't open to us. And with the amount of stuff we needed to rehome, it's unlikely they could have been much help anyway.

I also once heard about donations sitting outside the back door of a charity shop waiting for the bin men and that prompted me to look elsewhere for homes. Which led me to:

- Freegle
- Facebook Marketplace
- Ebay
- Emmaus
- homeless charities
- women's shelters
- local WhatsApp groups
- schools.

Freegle

I love Freegle[1]! If you're happy to give something away then this is your place. You can't charge for anything – hence their strapline 'like online dating for stuff.'

You can sign up with minimum fuss and make your first offering. Always include a picture so people can see if it's really what they want. Give as much detail as you can at the outset; it was measurements that got me – I kept forgetting to add them in. The more detail you include at the outset, the fewer questions you need to answer before you find a taker.

We moved many things through Freegle. Sometimes, I tried to sell elsewhere first, sometimes just gave away from the outset. We handed on everything from leftover pieces of tile from the new bathroom to an ice-cream maker to a wonderful wool-lined, silk curtain that had kept cold draughts at bay. The tiles became place settings for a kettle, cuppa and kitchen utensils, and the curtain was to be made into a bedspread. I met some lovely people, had interesting chats and enjoyed the feeling of just handing something over to a smiling face.

Facebook Marketplace

This works in a similar way to Freegle, but you can ask for payment. Of course you need a Facebook account, but once you have that you're on your way. You will find the link – Marketplace[2] – on the left-hand side of the page on your computer screen or at the foot of the mobile app – just click on that and you can have a mooch through and see how it works. When you're ready just click on 'create new listing' and post your item. Include a picture – to do this, click on 'add photos' for each picture you want to include and upload from there.

In my experience, most people will try to haggle or just offer less. It's up to you if you want to accept that. Often we did. On the few occasions when the interchange felt unpleasant, I said no and gave it away to someone who really wanted it.

It is also worth being aware that some people will want your stuff so they can sell it on. Again, it's up to you whether you're OK with that. The main clue, we decided, was that they were able to pick something up very quickly in their own van. There were moments when we had a lot of stuff that we needed out of the way so we were happy with that. Other times, when it was something that had been important to us, I preferred to see it go to someone who wanted it for themselves.

Local Facebook groups

Go looking on Facebook for local reuse and recycling groups. There you'll find people asking for stuff they want and letting people know what they have to give away. Check the rules of the specific group to find out if you can ask for money or not – they will vary as to how they function.

Ebay

Ebay[3] is a very popular way of selling things. I never tried it myself, but I know a lot of people who have used it successfully. It does offer the opportunity to sell items of value and to set up a bidding process that can increase the amount you get paid.

You have to have an account and be an approved Ebay seller. It's important to remember that Ebay covers the whole country. Unless you stipulate 'collection only' you will be responsible for transport/delivery of the item so make sure you include that cost in your asking price.

Emmaus

Emmaus[4] is a nationwide charity for the homeless that offers 'a home, meaningful work and a sense of belonging'. They sell furniture that's been renovated by residents of their communities and they will collect. They only take furniture that needs just a bit of work to make it useable, so be prepared that they may turn you down. But they are worth trying and they do great work.

Such interesting people

On a visit to India a few years ago, we bought a bolt of bright red gauze fabric, intending to hang it on the walls of our little pergola. It was a great idea, in theory, but we never really made it work. So there it was, sitting in the loft, totally forgotten – and perfect for Freegle.

Two days later a young woman arrived at the allotted time to gather it up. She was going to use it to make outfits for herself and her daughter. It reminded her of home, so there was a little tear shed, but then she walked away with a big smile on her face.

Then there were the offcuts of plasterboard. I never thought for one moment that anyone would want them, but just before they went in the skip I decided to give Freegle a try. They were one of our most popular offerings. It makes sense – imagine if you'd done most of your work and just needed one last bit of board. So much better to adopt someone's leftover bit than to buy a whole new sheet.

And the young man just setting up home with his girlfriend. They had nothing to sit on, so when he saw our reclining leather chairs on Facebook he was delighted. It took a few days to organise, but before long he was loading them into his van and driving them away to a new life.

One of my all-time favourites was putting my business books on Facebook. After 20 years of executive coaching I'd built up quite a library and a number of people wanted them. Some were clearly going to sell them on, so I passed. But then one young man told me he'd just completed his MBA and wanted to keep up his reading; a young mother running her own business wanted help with managing her team; and finally an interesting guy said quite clearly he was going to sell them to make money for his charity that supported kids struggling to stay out of trouble. I couldn't have been more delighted and I thoroughly enjoyed the conversations we had. Best outcome ever for books that served me well and would now help others.

————

Homeless charities

There are a number of organisations[5] in our hometown helping homeless people, in particular when someone is about to be given the key to their first home. At this point they have nothing, so it's a really positive way to hand on some of the stuff you no longer want or need. I've been particularly pleased when I've been able to hand on kitchen kit, bedding, rugs, lamps… to help someone build their first home. So find the best options near you and make contact. In my experience you will always be welcomed.

You may also find 'reuse' projects when items are cleaned up, mended or repurposed and offered for sale. This can also be a good place to find stuff you need yourself during the build, if you don't want to use your own favourites. As an example, look at this link[6].

If you can't find an actual website, try Facebook – they will probably have a page on there with plenty of information about what's needed.

Women's shelters

Women and children leaving a violent situation may have to walk away with nothing. So a women's shelter[7] is a perfect place to donate quality home items that have plenty of wear left in them. It will be the same process as for the homeless charities – go online and look for your local organisation; make contact and find out what they need and where you can drop off your offerings. Expect to meet up in a car park or local shopping centre. You will never be given the address of the shelter, for obvious reasons.

If you can't find a local website, then look on Facebook – they may well have their own page and someone else will certainly have asked the same question not so long ago.

Local WhatsApp groups

Loads of neighbourhood WhatsApp groups were set up during covid and many are still going strong. So if you are part of such a group, try putting up a post and offering items that might suit different age groups or people at different life stages. If anyone likes what you have to offer, it's the easiest option – it can be picked up from your doorstep or handed over alongside a cup of coffee.

Schools

Books, craft items and toys are often of value to schools. If you have your own kids or know someone with kids, you can easily find out what's needed. I've even been able to provide some interesting raffle prizes – that rather nice wine carafe that's never been used, for example.

LESSONS LEARNED

Binning is the last resort – you may have finished with something, but it will suit someone else perfectly. You just need to find them.

It might be a source of income – someone may be willing to pay for your surplus so it's always worth a try. If you can't find a buyer, then better to give it away to someone who needs it rather than send it to landfill.

Set your parameters – be clear from the outset - be clear whether you can deliver the item. Include its size in the listing and whether it needs a car or van, whether you can help carry stuff to a car or van, plus an honest summary of the condition.

Keep your options open until you see the whites of their eyes – some people are very respectful in this repurposing game, others are not. So never turn others away until you hand over the item. Instead, tell them someone is due to pick up the item and you'll let them know if they take it. Since buyers are often asked for comments about sellers, be respectful yourself, then people will be happy to wait and see.

Limit the number of offerings at one time – once interest begins it can be pretty intense for a time. I've had up to 10 people offering at once, which means keeping track of emails and requests. So take your time. No more than three things at one time and you'll be fine.

Never second guess what will be of interest - we thought we knew what would be of interest but were proved wrong so many times. So try anything you have and see what happens. Like the lovely, twice-used Samsonite suiter that eventually went to the charity shop, while the old TV wall bracket could have sold five times.

Be persistent – don't give up too easily – there will be more options than I've listed here, so go looking and see what you can find. Freecycle[8] and nextdoor[9] are just two more options I can think of.

Last resort options: skip hire, scrap metal person, recycling centre – make sure you know what will happen if you do have to dump. Some skip companies say they will recycle, so check that out when you book. The dump often has a recycling depot where they'll melt down the scrap metal, mulch wood etc. I had the scrap metal man on speed dial and he would come straight away to pick up.

Mindset change

This is all about a change in mindset. It's so tempting to see what we no longer want as 'rubbish'. But nowadays we finally understand how wrong landfill is. Now we are encouraged to limit consumption, buy second hand, repurpose and repair. So it's time to think differently and look first for who might want what you have.

Just to get you thinking, we sold or handed on:

- our complete kitchen and all appliances – even the wok hob
- our engineered wood floor
- the old back door
- a computer screen
- a sound system
- tap hoses
- white ornamental stones from the garden
- an unused loo seat
- a double skin radiator
- a leather sofa
- the old kettle
- plasterboard
- floorboards
- heavy duty builders bags
- spare tiles…

and that is just part of the list. Just imagine all that stuff sitting for hundreds of years polluting the planet. This way they'll do a much better job before they finally go to the place where such stuff goes to die.

SUMMARY

- Always look for other options before you dump your used stuff.
- Freegle and Facebook Marketplace are easy-to-use options that reach a lot of people.
- Your old waste may be just what someone else wants.
- Be clear about what you are offering and how much you can help at the pick-up.
- Always use a realistic picture in your ad – it helps people see what they are buying.
- You can sell your stuff and get a bit of income – as long as the price is right. Be ready to adjust to what the buyer will pay.
- You will meet some interesting people along the way.
- It's an interesting challenge and brings some variety into a dusty, builder-filled life.

---

1. http://www.ilovefreegle.org
2. https://www.facebook.com/marketplace/
3. https://www.ebay.co.uk
4. https://emmaus.org.uk/about-us
5. http://www.actionforhomeless.co.uk
6. http://www.hertfordshire.gov.uk/services/recycling-waste-and-environment/recycling-and-waste/where-can-i-recycle/reuse.aspx#whatis
7. bit.ly/3V7ekY6
8. https://www.freecycle.org/browse/UK/London
9. https://nextdoor.co.uk

AFTERWORD

WAS IT ALL WORTH IT?

Resounding answer: **YES!** Home is now a legacy – our offering to future generations. This book is the second part of the legacy. If I can get just one person to do the same, I will have achieved something.

BENEFITS

We have reduced our energy usage by 75%, so paying 25% of our previous bills.

Additional insulation keeps in the warmth. In recent excessive heat it also kept in the cool.

The house is significantly more comfortable than before.

We are less bothered by sound from outside.

The ASHP works well with little noise – no more than any heating system.

Heat exchange ventilation makes for a very comfortable fresh atmosphere in the house.

Solar power provides energy each day, not to mention the challenge – how can we make best use of the sunshine?

Warmth is steady throughout the day. No more rushing to the thermostat to turn the heating up because it's cold.

FINALLY

The satisfaction from doing a job that works well for us and works well for the earth is enormous.

GLOSSARY OF TERMS

ASHP - Air Source Heat Pump

Air bricks – Regular household bricks with holes in them for ventilation. Used primarily to create air flow underneath a suspended ground level timber floor to reduce condensation. **These must never be blocked up or covered.**

Batts – soft slabs of insulation material

Block and beam floor – floor made of suspended pre-cast concrete beams and blocks. The beam spans the space between the supporting walls with a lightweight concrete block as an infill

Breathability – The transfer of moisture through a material or building element.

Breathable paint – non toxic paint that is fully breathable with negligible VOC's, plastics or heavy metals. The final layer of a breathable wall.

COP – Coefficient of Performance. A measure of energy in compared to energy out. A high COP of 1:4 means you put in one unit of energy and get four units of energy out. 1:1 means you get just one until of energy out for every unit put in.

DCV – Demand-controlled ventilation. DCV can be combined with a smart home. If you have humidity sensors in your house, the DCV will extract the moist air when it is needed. This is a different system to MVHR, which runs constantly in the background.

DHW – domestic hot water

Diathonite – thermal plaster that can vary in thickness according to need. Diathonite can be used both internally and externally.

DPC - damp proof course.

DPM - damp proof membrane

Embodied energy – the amount of energy required to produce a product. High embodied energy means the item requires a lot of energy in its production, therefore less environmentally friendly. Low embodied energy is a feature of most eco products.

EnerPHit – "Quality-Approved Energy Retrofit with Passive House Components" Certificate. A set of standards to be achieved in an existing house so it has a high energy efficiency and reduced energy demands. If you want to reach EnerPHit levels discuss with your architect – measurements begin with the planning process so must be adhered to from the outset.

EPC – Energy Performance Certificate. Measurement of how energy efficient a home or a product is. Do be careful with this metric though, as it is a tick-box exercise and results can be misleading.

EPS – expanded polystyrene

Floating floor - floorboards are laid in an interlocking way over the floor, but not fixed down.

FENSA - certificate that confirms your window installer has complied with building regulations.

Loft legs – stands that raise your loft boarding above your insulation to allow storage without squashing/compressing which will compromise thermal performance and reduce effectiveness by over 50%.

Lime plaster – a traditional plaster used in old and eco buildings. Made of a mixture of lime, sand and water, lime plaster is breathable and eco friendly

LPG – Liquid Petroleum Gas

MEV – Mechanical extract ventilation

MVHR – Mechanical ventilation with heat recovery. MVHR is often a whole-house system that runs constantly in the background. It removes moist, stale air from the house and brings in fresh air. The air passes over a heat exchanger that transfers the heat from the outgoing air to the incoming air, helping to keep the house warm.

Off gassing – chemicals / pollutants that are released from petrochemical plastics in your home

PIR/PUR - rigid insulating material made using petrochemicals with high embodied energy. PIR has greater fire resistance than PUR. Brands include Kingspan and Celotex

Pressure gradient – air and/or moisture moving from higher to lower pressure. Particularly relevant to breathability.

PV – Photo voltaic solar panels that convert light into electric power

Renovation – to modify an existing house, or build a new part of the house from scratch: new extensions, opening up the loft in a house etc.

Retrofit – to improve or upgrade an existing building adding in systems that weren't there previously – insulation, PV/solar, ASHP etc.

R Value - the capacity of an insulating material to resist heat flow. The higher the R-value, the greater the insulating power.

Screed - a thin, top layer of material laid over a concrete subfloor, traditionally made of sharp sand and cement, similarly to concrete.

Sealing tape – strong, highly adhesive tape for sealing up joins between walls and windows, floor and walls. Important for air tightness.

Service penetrations – holes where services are brought into the house for electricity or water. Particularly important for air tightness – gaps between the hole in the wall and the relevant pipe will be a point of entry for draughts.

Service void – a space between the inner wall and the internal plasterboard. Used as a space for all the services to run – water pipes, electric cables etc. Stops the need for too many holes in the walls.

Solar heat gain – the amount of heat that your windows allow into the room. Low SHG increases comfort levels in summer by reducing the heat that comes in

Sub floor void – the gap between the earth and the joists under a suspended floor. Important for air bricks to be unimpeded in the void to avoid condensation and mould

Suspended wood floor – a floor that is supported on timber joists, with a void below.

Thermal bridge, cold bridge - an object or part of an object which has higher thermal conductivity than the surrounding materials and hasn't been fully insulated. This means that heat is lost and there is a risk of moisture condensing on the colder surface, leading to mould.

Thermal Imaging camera – a handheld device that detects infrared energy (heat) and converts it into an image. Thermal cameras are used for troubleshooting eg: identifying cold spots, poorly fitting windows, inadequate insulation……..

U Value – measures the heat lost through a given material, or group of materials that form a building element (such as a wall, roof or floor). Used to describe efficiency of insulation materials and double/triple glazing etc.

UFH - Underfloor heating

VOC – volatile organic compounds. Invisible gases that build up from cosmetics, air fresheners, hair spray, cleaning fluids and off gassing, the chemicals released from plastics in your home.

Wood fibre insulation - robust and flexible insulation that can be used for floors, roofs and walls. It is recyclable, locks in carbon as it grows and is relatively free of pollutants. It also has low U values and is 100% compostable and recyclable at the end of its life

INDEX

ABOUT THE AUTHOR

Eco renovation has become my retirement focus. After a long career helping people achieve their best – psychotherapy, then executive coaching and leadership development – I've doubled down on environment and climate. Always important to me, now an imperative, I want there to be a liveable world for all our kids to enjoy.

It is a major change for me, yet it fits perfectly with my own theory of success[1] – the life alignment curve:

- Restlessness - I didn't know what to do when work stopped. No idea what I was going to do with the rest of my life. Being granny is the best occupation ever, but there is room for more.
- Incubation - so I sat with the dilemma. Sometimes calmly, often frustrated, occasionally excited.
- Epiphany - finally the penny dropped. I care so deeply about the earth, but I'll never be a direct action person – I don't have the courage. But I do understand eco renovation, which is a great way to take personal direct action. I know I can write – done it before – so why not write the laypersons' guide so others can also take direct action and create their own heritage house for the future.
- Drive - and once I decided, I was off like a rocket. Lots to learn, understand, explore.

I hope the result is useful for you. May you enjoy the process and gain huge satisfaction from the end result. The earth thanks you!

This may be my last iteration of the life alignment curve or there may be more to come – who knows.

Follow progress on my blog[2]: ecorenovationhome.com

1. https://www.whsmith.co.uk/products/the-psychology-of-success-secrets-of-serial-achievement/judith-learyjoyce/paperback/9780273720898.html?gclid=EAIaIQobChMIgKDryceH-QIVwoBQBh0idwbbEAQYAyABEgIKKfD_BwE&gclsrc=aw.ds
2. ecorenovationhome.com